Ernest Buckler

CRITICAL VIEWS ON CANADIAN WRITERS

MICHAEL GNAROWSKI, *Series Editor*

Other titles in preparation

CRITICAL VIEWS ON CANADIAN WRITERS

Ernest Buckler

Edited and with an Introduction by
GREGORY M. COOK

MICHAEL GNAROWSKI, Series Editor

McGRAW-HILL RYERSON LIMITED

TORONTO • MONTREAL • NEW YORK • LONDON • SYDNEY

JOHANNESBURG • MEXICO • PANAMA • DÜSSELDORF • SINGAPORE

RIO DE JANEIRO • KUALA LUMPUR • NEW DELHI

ERNEST BUCKLER

ISBN 0-07-092958-0
Library of Congress Catalog Card Number 72-1350
Printed and bound in Canada
1 2 3 4 5 6 7 8 9 0   AP-72   0 9 8 7 6 5 4 3 2

Grateful acknowledgment is made to the following for permission to
quote: to Hugh MacLennan and The Macmillan Company of Canada
Limited for an extract from *Each Man's Son;* to Northrop Frye and
Princeton University Press for two passages from *Anatomy of Criticism;*
to Sinclair Ross and McClelland and Stewart Limited for an extract
from *As For Me and My House* and to Irving Layton and McClelland
and Stewart Limited for lines from the poem "The Birth of Tragedy."

Extracts from *The Mountain and the Valley, The Cruelest Month* and
Ox Bells and Fireflies are reprinted by permission of Ernest Buckler and
The Canadian Publishers McClelland and Stewart Limited, Toronto.

For Miriam

CONTENTS

INTRODUCTION

*My commandments are sewn into my skin: if I go for a
day without writing the scar burns me; and if I write too
easily, it also burns me.*

Sartre, Words

I

Sartre's words are an extract of the physical urge that has
obsessed Ernest Buckler. This collection of criticism maps the
metaphysics of that urge through its cyclic pattern as it emerges
in the three works of fiction. David Canaan, artist-hero of
The Mountain and the Valley (1952), wears the external scar
of his burning headache; Paul Creed, "co-author" of *The
Cruelest Month* (1963), carries the pain of the "notifying"
heartache internally and remains an enigma—protected from
the commiserate look of others—because he lacks the external
scar; Paul's co-author is Morse Halliday who, facing the death
of his talent, cannot resist the "selfish plan engendered in him
by another's tragedy" and even tells us how he will write the
book we have just read. And he "spoke stridently, but somehow ineptly with heartsickness, as if he were parodying a
parody of himself." It is Morse Halliday who must be used
as the supervisor of any collective thesis on Ernest Buckler's
work. Morse, and the thesis on writing, in *The Cruelest Month,*
create the pivot point of the cycle of work that culminates
with *Ox Bells and Fireflies* (1968). David Canaan, whose scar
of experience marks both fallen man and the appointed one,
dies before he can write the book that will radiate the neglected
warmth in the lives of his family and friends who have been

1

visited by tragedy, before he can give the "absolving voice to all the hurts they gave themselves or each other." This was the commandment sewn into his skin. It was also his redemption. It was the legacy he left Paul Creed. But Paul had a self-contempt for this selfish plan. He had a second closely allied inhibition.

He caught himself close to the wispily elegiac plaintiveness that unconsciously poeticizes itself, frighteningly close to rehearsing his deprivation with that toxic "lingering" regard of the self-commiserative. It was the thing more than anything in God's world he loathed.

Although Paul, like David, had the "shriving clarity when you've first come face-to-face with mortal threat," he could not write the novel. And he would hold Morse's novel in contempt.

Buckler has said that *The Mountain and the Valley* was the novel he *had* to write ("My First Novel"). He said that in *The Cruelest Month* he attempted too much, as "in every novel one is perennially tempted to cover everything so that it will no longer be necessary to write another " ("My Second Book"). That "everything" included David Canaan's promise to radiate the "soundness of the 'natural' country person," but Buckler admits, after the publication of *The Cruelest Month,* "I'm not all so sure about this now. Not at all." With the publication of *Ox Bells and Fireflies* it is finally clear that all the masks of the artist hero are dropped and Buckler is freed from the narrative history that creates the essential reality of the first book—the novel; and freed from the artificiality of the types in symposium in the second book—the anatomy; and, finally, he redeems David, Paul, Morse and the natural country life in the "fictional memoir"—the confession— of "the way it was."

It is essential to recognize that Buckler has written three works of prose fiction.[1] The first is a *novel* that deals with personality in the framework of a stable society. Although the

---

[1] See "Specific Continuous Forms (Prose Fiction)," by Northrop Frye. In *Anatomy of Criticism* (Princeton, New Jersey: Princeton University Press, 1957), pp. 303-14.

particular rural village society and the key personality psycho-analyzed are under attack, they are recognized as conventional. In the second work, what appears to be the romancer's escape from conventional attitudes in the portrayal of individualized and idealized characters in a nihilistic world is, in fact, an *anatomy*. This form tends toward intellectual analysis. Five "types" of characters, representing five levels of society in the outside (conventional) world, are brought to the rural setting of Endlaw where they conduct a symposium. The third work is clearly a *confession*. This form frees Buckler from the continuous narrative that requires theory to be dissolved into personal relationships and it frees him from the masked narrator who, as Morse Halliday insists, must see everything through a "squint." Buckler finds in the third form the convention appropriate for the integrating process of the earlier work that finally confirms for him that *his* life is worth writing about. Both he and the reader are sure now that the natural country persons, "however inchoate their expression sometimes was, were as charged with depths and intricacies of thought and feeling as the more sophisticated" ("My Third Book").

A study of Buckler's life will show that his writing is not literally autobiographical, "except as all writing is . . . between the lines . . . autobiographical." Therefore, a reading of Buckler's three major works involves a trip: with David Canaan in search of his paradise[2] as he comes to grips with the *flesh* translating itself through experience of youth en route to isolation; with Paul Creed in dissection of the *bones* of life, in the cerebral sense, from isolation to old age, continuing through the contemplative record of the *spirit* of "the way it was." This is the cyclic pattern of Buckler's anagoge as well as the pattern of each of the individual works—from the "happy valley" (Entremont) of wonder, through the "no where" (Endlaw) of

---

[2] "Image and Symbol in the Fiction of Ernest Buckler," by Bernita Harris, an unpublished Master's thesis, Library, University of New Brunswick, 1969, provides an interesting study of this pattern in the second book (the search for the Holy Grail) in her elaborate study of the cross-references (deliberate and unconscious) between *The Cruelest Month* and *The Wasteland* that demonstrates Buckler and T. S. Eliot as pebbles in the same stream.

experience, to return to the "no more place" (Norstead) in the fictive memoir world of innocence. The biographical revelation of Buckler's creed and the exposition of his craft is organically, rather than artificially, structured. The short stories, not dealt with in detail in this volume (nor yet available in collection), the articles, letters and reviews prove to be the templets that create a pattern for testing the accuracy of this form. Therefore, neither a résumé of biography nor a paraphrase of Buckler's self-criticism is necessary here. What is required is a thread to relate Buckler and his three major works of prose fiction to the criticism of his work to date.

Through the efforts of agent Henry Ober and Associates and Henry Holt and Company in New York, Buckler's career (with considerable cost and care) was allowed a meteoric launching in the United States. Sterling North's column in the New York *World-Telegram and Sun,* November 7, 1952, cast orchids to two novelists: "To Hemingway for his comeback with *The Old Man and the Sea,*" and to "Ernest Buckler, a Nova Scotian farmer, who against tremendous odds, loneliness, poverty, and back-breaking labor has come through with a fresh and exciting first novel, *The Mountain and the Valley.*" It is not surprising, therefore, that Sheila spars with Morse by telling him the truth in *The Cruelest Month:* "Whenever one of your books did come out there always seemed to be a Hemingway—or a Faulkner—or something such that one *must* read . . . ."

To the critics who met the honoured guest at a P.E.N. party in New York, the bachelor-farmer-philosopher from Nova Scotia was unique. They were anxious to give "The See-saw of a Writer's Luck"[3] a boost. They were familiar with his work in *Coronet, Esquire, Ladies Home Journal, Atlantic* and *Maclean's.* Major newspapers carried a piece by Buckler which described the books in his life, in particular what Ernest Hemingway, Elizabeth Bowen, Henry James and Marcel Proust meant to him.

---

[3] "The See-saw of a Writer's Luck," by Ernest Buckler. In *Quill and Quire,* October 1952, pp. 28, 32.

The reviews proliferated, calling him the Thomas Hardy of Nova Scotia, a Willa Cather for dignity and homespun beauty, a Mary Webb and a Thomas Wolfe. Then came the allusions to Jane Austen and D. H. Lawrence. What in New York was called "a delicate subject," "rich and earthy" in New England, became "objectionable" in Kansas. "Fornication between twelve-and fourteen-year-olds is going rather far" (Dallas). The "pleasing, moving farm chronicle," which made radio critics (who, Buckler believed, had not read the novel) "weep," is found to have some "painfully fancy writing." The 1952 euphemism for writing about sex as a martial force is "excessive preoccupation with bodily and biological details."[4]

The result of all this was the sale of 7,000 copies of the *original* hardcover edition and a sale of pocket book rights to the New American Library of World Literature (while Buckler was in New York for the three-week promotion). This resulted in a 150,000-copy edition under the Signet Classics imprint in 1954 (with a jacket design suggesting love on the farm), which sold out. It also resulted in Buckler's return to the farm at Centrelea, Nova Scotia—contrary to the usual self-depreciating assumptions by literary people in Canada that he would move to New York—where he began writing *The Cruelest Month* and put into Morse Halliday's mouth:
What's all this ruckus about good taste . . . when what's good taste in one longitude is anathema in another? . . . O Yes, these critics were a choice gallery all right.

It is a more sympathetic gallery of critics that are collected here; most of them have that "milk of human kindness" Morse said was lacking when they recognized the "writer's guts riddled." It is by coincidence, however, that only one of those hundreds of American reviews that were so good for the sale of the book is included here; it is the first in the collection and it is written by a Canadian.[5]

---

[4] The climate of the book's reception (suggested by these gems from newspaper clippings) is perhaps best illustrated by the reminder that the rather innocent movie *The Moon Is Blue* first defied the censors' ban in 1952.
[5] Stuart Keate was editor of the *Daily Times,* Victoria, B.C.

"But surely," Kate said, "you're not Gulliver. Pigmies you despise like that—surely you shouldn't let anything they say bind you down and silence you? You wouldn't *want* their kiss of death, would you?"

Buckler, through Morse, is reacting cynically to the "social" responsibility this kind of criticism demands of himself and the writer. It is undoubtedly responsible in part for Buckler's decision to abandon the reflection of real society in his second book and provide instead an anatomy through the Endlaw symposium.[6]

"My First Novel" could not be more sympathetic. The novelist himself raises the key issues to be dealt with by the critics in the first third of this volume. The purgatorial image of the author is the one introduced by Buckler's opening essay.

Stuart Keate's review is representative because it recognizes the employment of symbol, dream, bucolic environment and over-ripe language, but fails to appreciate the internal action of the psychological novel and mistakenly calls the narrative uneven and formless. William Arthur Deacon promptly balances the perspective. He sees the significance wrung from the trivial and thereby lends the lever to later critics who recognize Buckler's realistic approach in raising the would-be parochial to the universal level. S. Morgan-Powell's review is one of the most perceptive among the early newspaper pieces because it places *The Mountain and the Valley* properly in its socio-historical context of the receding farming frontier in Canadian society.

Katherine Douglas's distinction between her reading of the novel and "the general reading public" taste in 1952 signals the last word by Harry Brown who says that the "Average Reader" may not be equipped to digest Buckler's prose. More importantly, she seems to sense the tensions between the images of gloom and joy D. O. Spettigue refers to fifteen years later in "The Way It Was." Similarly, she seems to anticipate the attitudes of *threat, haven* and *potential* that Spettigue argues

---

[6] It is worth noting here that the allusion to Swift's satire, not to mention encylopaedias, Huxley and the *Book of Common Prayer,* early in *The Cruelest Month* is a clue to Buckler's interest in the anatomy.

are embodied in Canadian literature and, indeed, epitomized in Buckler's fiction.

Her question about the missing link in David Canaan's life (adolescence to early middle age) as it distracts from the development of the plot is useful. It is a reminder that Buckler, during that interval, had left the rural setting to study at Dalhousie University in Halifax and the University of Toronto, and to work as an actuary for Manufacturers' Life in Toronto. If Morgan-Powell is correct about the migration of the rural person to the urban setting, then Buckler's portrait of the *village* life will not be able to reflect the most likely transient, the precocious young adult. The flaw, if it is a flaw, is found both in the fictional and in the non-fictional life of the community. It recalls R. E. Watters' thesis that the author cannot be expected to reflect what is unknown in the community.

Claude Bissell's review provides an approach to the novel that might compensate for the flaw. His emphasis on the portrait of human relations in the family distracts from the second purpose—the portrait of the artist as a young man. Of course, the hero's search for identity does run parallel to the family's growth in the first half of the novel, and his wounding awareness of his potential is a rapid result, in the second half of the novel, of his family group's disintegration.

What Keate called formless is recognized by Bissell as a "triumph over linear time." His suggestion of the importance of the isolation and relation to environment themes in connection with W. O. Mitchell and Sinclair Ross anticipates Warren Tallman's exploration of these three, and two other Canadian authors, in "Wolf in the Snow."

From 1953 to 1960 Buckler's reputation grew by word of mouth. R. E. Watters, as public lecturer, attracted audiences by offering Hugh MacLennan and Mazo de la Roche on a bill-of-fare that included Buckler for desert. His treatment of *The Mountain and the Valley* appears in print for the first time in this collection. He is bold in his praise of the novel (only two years after its publication) and bold in his critical approach. He articulates Buckler's use of two devices that enrich the universal truth of the novel—that every moment of our lives is the cumulative total of every preceding moment. The first device, of course, is the presentation of the entire narrative as a moment of the same day, that day represented in prologue and epilogue. The second device, as subtly deployed under the reader's feet as the rug she hooks, is the protagonist's grandmother, Ellen, who "destroys the leavings of the past in order to incorporate them into the pattern of the present . . . like a deity in an ancient myth bending over the web of time." Without hesitating to worry about the novel's easier mark as a regional piece of literature, Watters recognizes David Canaan's hoped-for function as a master artist, a novelist of national character and universal humanity. The irony of Watters' preoccupation with Buckler's novel is that its community of humanity, presumably from rural Nova Scotia—a life style supposedly disappearing—is, in fact, a replica of the larger Canadian community, including the audience at this lecture in Victoria and Nanaimo, because it is a community of people whose "sensory response is blunted by utility and erased by custom," a community whose literature is unknown. As Watters suggests in the subsequent article, it is a community that may not deserve the literature it gets. David Canaan's death then at the moment of his realization of his function is the epitome of that irony, that myth of Canadian and human society.

Watters' definition of, and rationalization for, David's sensitivity keened by community rather than landscape (which really becomes the objective correlative between artist-narrator-hero and reader) does not contradict Tallman's wolf-in-snow thesis, but it shifts the emphasis enough to remind us of the novelist's role as a functionary of community. It is this role that requires the would-be poet of landscape and the lyricist of the human heart to work in a continuous specific form of fiction (the novel).

R. E. Watters' "Unknown Literature" marks the turning point in Canadian letters and reflects Buckler's relationship to the general change of climate. Not only does he introduce what was perhaps the most influential anthology in Canadian university courses for the following ten years, but his allusion to the *Report* of the Massey Commission conjures up many similar articles that resulted in such phenomena as The Canadian Writers' Conference held at Queen's University in 1955. The remainder of this collection of criticism might be considered an indirect consequence of that conference. For The Canada Council (founded in 1959) was to foster Buckler, some of the contributors, and some of the magazines from which these reviews and articles were gleaned (e.g. *Canadian Literature*).

Watters' rhetoric of "this Promised Land," "Canadian national character" and "natural resources," and his images of the complex human being and the novelist's difficulty in recognizing him in what still seems to be a frontier society echo the search for identity in relation to landscape that Warren Tallman follows with in 1960. Watters' singling out of Buckler's *The Mountain and the Valley* as an example of what may be better than the Canadian reader deserves, is prophetic of the highest praise to be given Buckler some fourteen years later. What amounts almost to an innuendo about the failure of scholarship is promptly confirmed by an examination of Buckler's second book and promptly challenged by the major pieces in the remainder of this volume.

"Why should we Canadians demand a masterpiece in every little hill we hoe?" he asks. As Tallman opens his study of David,

. . . he finds himself inched unwillingly away from others onto a precarious plane of solitary being from which he can communicate his extravagant reactions only by other extravagances which further emphasize his growing isolation,

images of the commandment and the scar reverberate. It also recalls the opening of a poem by John Newlove:

> Everyone is so
> lonely in this
> country that
> it's necessary
> to be fantastic.

II

A rationale for *The Cruelest Month* as a gondola between the
two books that will continue to be recognized as pinnacles in
Canadian Literature—*The Mountain and the Valley* and *Ox
Bells and Fireflies*—can be developed. *The Cruelest Month*
manifests two kinds of isolation. The first is the isolation of
the author from any useful criticism of his craft and points
toward a failure of Canadian criticism;[7] the second is Buckler's
own choice of the role of *isolé* so that the kinds of characters
portrayed in the anatomy represent the only kind who seek
out the isolé. Unless he is to return to the original experience—
satisfactorily handled in the first book, the novel—he must
write about his new experience. This involves the cast at
Endlaw. The question must be answered: why did Buckler
write about writing in *The Cruelest Month?* After all, it was
Buckler who said in 1952 ("My First Novel"):

. . . when writers associate too much with each other, a sort
of inbreeding starts to develop. You half-hear them saying:
Now we'll form a hermetically sealed little group, and the
password will be Yoknapatawpha, or Anna Livia Plurabelle, or
something, eh?—And so on. Which is disastrous. And eventually they may come to write almost entirely about writing.
Which is ruinous. At best, writing is only shadow. Writing about
writing, then, is a dim second carbon indeed.

As a matter of fact, almost every point raised by Buckler in
"My First Novel" as he braced himself against puritanical
outrage, faking Canadianism, exposure of juvenile indiscretions,
his lack of interest in the action novel, and writing about
writing are dissected in *The Cruelest Month* by one of the

---

[7] The criticism of Warren Tallman (1960) appeared after *The Cruelest
Month* was cast, that of D. O. Spettigue (1967) after *Ox Bells and
Fireflies* was set, and the four Masters' theses appeared in Canadian
libraries after the publication of the last book.

writing, reading or spectator characters. It was not the critical acclaim and financial success that helped Buckler produce the second and third books. Those circumstances only produced the cynical ultra-ego, Morse. It was the changing atmosphere in Canada that saw the latter works completed. More sympathetic *and* responsible criticism and patronage made it possible for Buckler's work to climax with the potential second classic of its kind: *Ox Bells and Fireflies*. This does not imply, however, that criticism has even yet fulfilled its promise. So far it is primarily the latent criticism (unpublished theses) that has recognized the breakthrough in *The Mountain and the Valley*'s synthesis of the mainstreams in Canadian literature and its particular contribution to the future of the realistic novel. Nor does it demonstrate, except for the hint R. G. Baldwin offers in his review and the care Spettigue takes with what is so far the most important single piece of criticism on Buckler, that *The Cruelest Month* has been recognized on its own merits as an anatomy instead of a novel. And it does not suggest the importance of *Ox Bells and Fireflies* as a confession, except that Buckler has been taken at his word that it is important to record a way of life that is vanishing (or has vanished) forever.

Baldwin opens his review:

Few reviewers will risk a prose flourish at the expense of this painfully honest book. Buckler will have the skin off anyone who goes for an easy mark, anyone, including himself.

Later he recognizes the peculiar value of the book, especially Morse

. . . who, in expounding his creed, tells us more about the writer's craft than most anthologies on the subject. If Buckler ever gets to the point of being fair game for "studies," this book will be a godsend to the scholars undertaking them, for the creed expounded is obviously Buckler's own, and the book discussed by his novel-writing character is, just as obviously, this one.[8]

---

[8] It is interesting to note that Baldwin refers to *The Cruelest Month* as a "book" and never as a novel.

It is apparent that Buckler's impatience with criticism led him to what would be a dim carbon in the novel, but it also led him to a book which might not be as dim as Robert Harlow suggests if it were recognized on its own merits. *The Cruelest Month* is in the Canadian tradition of Susanna Moodie's *Roughing It in the Bush,* James De Mille's *A Strange Manuscript Found in a Copper Cylinder* and Frederick Philip Grove's *In Search of Myself.* Mrs. Moodie told us of the lack of literate criticism in Canada and the plight of the writer; presumably this is why her apprenticeship novel was a far better book than the novels which followed. De Mille employs the conventions of the anatomy that Buckler's second book tends toward. And Grove explained the point at hand in *In Search of Myself:*

Just as a tree, falling in virgin forest, out of earshot of man or beast, does not produce a sound but merely wave-like disturbance of the air, thus writing which finds no reader does not produce art, which is in its very nature a reaction. I likened my work to such a tree falling; its sound arises merely in the nerve centres of him who hears. . . .

"My second Book" is reminiscent of both Paul's and Morse's notes on their would-be books as they are transcribed in *The Cruelest Month.* Its most obvious link with Bissell's review is the proposed title, "The Cells of Love." Bissell describes the book as a "study in the various kinds of love" in all the stubbornness suggested by Buckler's further dual definition of "cells" as both the constituent parts and the place of incarceration.

Bissell links the first two books, particularly their study of the group. His use of the "farmhouse philosopher" phrase recalls the caricature the U.S. newspapers drew of Buckler in 1952. His admission that the more complex, intense and involved prose exemplifies the obsession of great writers sets the tone of the second part of this volume.

Robert Harlow makes Bissell's remark that the characters do *not* spring naturally to life appear as gross understatement.

While no one until Spettigue's article notes the deviation from the novelist's approach, Bissell does say that Buckler pressurizes his characters by putting them in isolation. Harlow mentions Huxley, but he obviously insists that both Huxley and Buckler write a novel and not even an anatomy that tends to be a novel. His remark that Buckler uses language well is its own kind of understatement.

Jack Sheriff's review, however, puts the emphasis more properly on the importance of place and man circumscribed by the environment as symbolized by the fire. It is worthy of note that, despite David Canaan's reference to E. M. Forster and Buckler's acknowledgement of him in "My First Novel," Sheriff is the only critic to examine Buckler in terms of Forster's influence. The same critic also recognizes Buckler's deliberate use of the Hegelian dialectic.

While both R. G. Baldwin and F. W. Watt veil their remarks with the summation phrases "great, if unresolved, power" and "powerful imagination, however cramped and inhibited it so often is," the first is praise and the second expressed disappointment. Watt's disappointment is related, of course, to the theme he feels Buckler is exploring: "the price of detachment and independence."

Among the many other things it does (mentioned elsewhere in this introduction), Spettigue's article captures the representative Buckler activity of reminiscing about the hurting and healing power of love. His article becomes prophetic, therefore, of *Ox Bells and Fireflies* and the unifying vision attempted there through the return to the world of innocence and wonder. Of course, his heraldry of David Canaan's Canadian literary family, which includes Susanna Moodie, Grove's Len Sterner, Knister's Richard Milne, Robertson Davies' Monica Gall and Ross's Philip Bentley, expands the house already examined and possessed by Tallman. Spettigue also notes the characteristic ties of the romance discernible in *The Cruelest Month* and their significance in Buckler's other work.

Alden Nowlan's letter is a buffer between the middle and the last section of this collection of criticism. It demonstrates,

as perhaps Brown's letter to the Alfred Knopf editor and Spet-
tigue's article will, the potential of Buckler as a writer's writer.
These three men are established writers of fiction, two of them
Buckler's junior.

III

Baldwin's skin-off-the-nose image and Grove's nerve centres
(Marshall McLuhan would say) bring back the Sartrian image
of the commandment and the scar. If Buckler's commandment
was to create the finely textured pattern of "the way it was"
in *Ox Bells and Fireflies,* his particular obsession was with
style. It would be through style he would scar the nerve
centres of his reader once he had found the appropriate pattern.
Spettigue's article traces that urge and the tension evoked in
the contrasting emotions of gloom and joy.[9] The gloom and
the joy are reflected in the impending fate implied by the scar
and the promise of the mark of the appointed one.

The "it" of "the way it was" is the meanest of terms but on it
is placed the burden of conveying the most transcendent experiences of unity in the fleeting moment. Against the memories
of ecstatic experiences of wholeness are set those of separation,
dissolution and alienation, and these are associated with guilt
at the failure to seize the offered moment in which harmony
might have been restored. The "was" of the phrase thus represents a complex of times in which the moment being lived by
the character is contrasted with an ideal might-have-been which
in turn is extracted from the recollection of an actual "was" of
the character's past.

Spettigue's relation of this recurrent phrase, "the way it was,"
in Buckler's fiction to what he identifies as three fundamental
attitudes in Canadian fiction—the *threat,* the *haven,* the *poten-*

---

[9] The images of joy (of the conquered vision from the mountain, of the
memory of April and the flashes of fireflies) and the gloom (of the
suffocating valley, of the cruel desire of April and the sorrowful
sound of ox bells) are seen in the Buckler titles.

tial—and his development of this approach is extremely incisive. It might further be suggested that Buckler's three books have these three attitudes at their centre in the same progression.

Spettigue sees time (was) and place (it) as the essential grids in Buckler's work. But he does not interpret the "way" of the phrase; "way," of course, represents (or commands) the style with which the author will deal with the "it" and "was" of the phrase. The grid points will only be aligned through the "way" and this depends upon the appropriateness of style.

Frye may help us specify the forms of world literature, and their conventions, with which Buckler works. Tallman and Spettigue (with the help of Roy Daniells, D. G. Jones and the reviewers in this collection) may help to specify the peculiar North American and Canadian attitudes in which the forms define themselves. Ultimately, however, the individual writer's size as a pebble in the stream of the tradition will be determined by his special style. It was, of course, Buckler's facility with language that launched his writing career by winning a *Coronet* writing contest and by publication of early stories (in magazines such as *Esquire*) between 1938 and 1946. Style is the scar that will mark Buckler among or apart from other writers.

William Arthur Deacon recognized what he called a "poetic prose." The *Savannah News* (December 14, 1952) summed up its review:

The prose has a cleanliness about it, an inexorable decisiveness which lends peculiar eloquence . . . there is a feeling here of a heart purged of anguish through incisive, articulate delineation of experience.

Both Katherine Douglas and Deacon noted the bare bones rather than the abstract technique of the stream-of-consciousness portrayal of thought process "with the clinical skill of a biologist dissecting a frog"; Deacon adds, "It is literary psychoanalysis and physical dissection." He goes on to point out, however, that (as with Henry James) it can be wearying picking up the countless nuances. In the context of a discussion of his third book in 1967 Buckler said, "These people and their *happenings* . . . I was having happenings before they knew what they were." David Canaan expresses it on his mountain climb in the epilogue.

He could think of anything now. Everything seemed to be an aspect of something else. There seemed to be a thread of similarity running through the whole world. A shape could be like a sound; a feeling like a shape; a smell the shadow of a touch . . . His senses seemed to run together.

If the ultimate goal of Buckler is to portray the soundness of the natural country people, and that "however inchoate their expression sometimes was, they were as charged with depths and intricacies of thought and feeling as the more sophisticated," then (like David) his scar is a burning symbol and fact that he must perfect the "supreme gift" of evocation of "half-forgotten but instantly recognized pictures, odors, feelings, thoughts and impressions" which are the product of the disciplined innate ear and mind. With a native, but trained, ear for dialogue and the secret senses of the human spirit, his immersion in mathematics and philosophy (so integral to his prose style) works hand-in-hand to seek the symmetry of exactness and equation of truly "the *way* it was."

Claude Bissell calls this the "high metaphysical style" essential to the psychological novel and a rarity in Canadian fiction. Spettigue calls Buckler's style the language of simile. He sees the basis of the similes as the division of personality which has its counterpart in the divisions of *The Mountain and the Valley*. It also becomes apparent that this division of personality is countered in Paul Creed, the introverted would-be author, and Morse Halliday, the extroverted novelist, in *The Cruelest Month*. As Spettigue recognizes, words are David's *potential* for redemption, but he lacks the unifying symbol (like that his grandmother finds in her rug) and even at the moment of faith at his *haven* at the top of the mountain he is overcome by the *threat* of an unintelligible landscape. But this tableau of faith, hope and love works itself out in Buckler's three books. The threat of the unintelligible landscape, that stifles David at the moment he realizes that the *faithful* can be redeemed by love, does not threaten Paul and Morse during their escape to the haven of Endlaw. Paul has *hope* for the potential of words, but he abandons it because he cannot escape that commiserate squint he must adopt as narrator; Morse has lost *hope* for his potential with words, except through that cynical squint he epitomizes. It is not landscape but identity of self that threatens here. The potential is most fully challenged by Buckler in *Ox Bells and Fireflies*. For it is in the confession that the impossible rug-hooking of narrative into a suitable symbol to make the landscape intelligible is abandoned, along with the unsatisfactory pity that David and Paul would evoke as central identities (and the cynicism of Morse) in favour of the lens of *love* that David had promised to use to radiate the way it was. Landscape patterns have been abandoned, self has been allowed to escape and *Ox Bells and Fireflies* must rise or fall primarily on the merits of its style, the texture of an inscape perhaps. This entire argument seems to suggest Buckler has written his last major work of fiction. The cycle seems complete. However, one would have thought this, as Buckler hoped, when *The Cruelest Month* appeared. If the tableau of this introduction is too simple and too complete to be accurate, then Buckler may attempt to top the confession. I hesitate to suggest the direction he will take next. The three books were unpredictable, yet so obvious in retrospect.

Buckler's role in this study of his work is obvious now. His "My Third Book" announces the final section of this volume that will deal with his paradise regained in art, if lost in life.

The confession, *Ox Bells and Fireflies,* is dedicated to Claude Bissell and it takes little imagination to see him as "the professor" portrayed in the book. This may make Bissell the sympathetic critic he is, but it does not make him nonobjective. He spots the islands of happiness and despair placed side by side in the book. What he called a triumph over linear time in the first novel now becomes a despising of time by Buckler.

He reads the rare metaphysical style as "tuned" this time: the language is not of what things are like, but what they are. There is no longer the guilt-tenseness about the language of simile Spettigue defined earlier.

My own review allows that Buckler has fulfilled David Canaan's obsession to possess the thing, to get it outside himself. I see the same "pool of deep recognition" Liselotte Berliner sees, the mystic unity achieved through love. Buckler escapes what Desmond Pacey calls the "saccharinely sentimental" through feeling which Buckler says is the only thing that "saves us *at all* . . . and it seems to me you just bloody well go ahead and feel. And never mind what people say."[10] (The squint that Paul Creed feared is dismissed.)

Miss Berliner identifies the regular cycle of nature and the elemental game of chance, but Buckler's world is clearly inhabited by natural people who have not been destroyed because they have not hardened to sentiment.

Spettigue recognizes the introverted and intellectual characteristic of the confession of a lifetime's wisdom. Spettigue now sees that Buckler's style goes beyond telling it *like* it was: "he puts you 'right there' . . . 'Down we went,' as Eliot says, but we can still at intervals catch glimpses of the garden."

Perhaps what Wallace Stevens recognized in Eliot might also be seen in Morse, when Stevens's haunting line is recalled: "A dead romantic is a falsification."

CONCLUSION

When Kate reads Morse's flippant remarks about literature in a newspaper interview, she feels he is creating a self-caricature. She thinks:

[10] See "Canadian Prose and Verse," a review of *Ox Bells and Fireflies* by Donald Cameron; in *Queen's Quarterly* 76 (Autumn 1969), pp. 546-47.

Each in His Narrow Cell hadn't sounded that way. The first novel had been savage enough, but it was the savagery of compassion. She'd detected a change in his second, *The Cock Crew Thrice*. It was like derisive grinding on a festered tooth, an animal biting its own wound. Now she detected that change sharper still. What had happened to him?

The image of the wound in Morse is savage. The commandment that he write his book, despite the impending death of his talent, is as bad as this. Late in *The Cruelest Month* there is an exchange between Kate and Morse:

"My, we *are* death on heroes, aren't we?" Kate said, with the purposely ambiguous smile that can either disarm the remark or hone it.

"Not alto*gether*," Morse said. "Not quite, I've decided to spare a couple. This old clown here—" he nodded at Paul— "and myself . . ."

Paul, unlike David, recovers from his heart attack. He asks to see four more seasons. Before the book's resolution he sums up:

And I thought I was some kind of hero, he pressed the challenge. Oh yes, I did. Not consciously; but underneath somewhere I had the picture of myself. The old inviolate, self-sufficient, nohow seducible hero. Oh, I've really tricked myself ten ways from Sunday.

Paul's resolution (including marriage to Letty) is not so total as David's. But it is complemented by Morse's. Like David, Paul has had his group (family) and let them go. He has had them long enough to assess accurately his own position and shatter his delusion of being the invincible hero. In the book's final paragraph, however, Paul feels the David-kind of "inimitable safety":

. . . that great, sweet, wonderful safety from the cry of things not understood, of things said and things not said, of things done and not done, of what is near and what far-off, and the sound of time and the sound of time gone by . . . .

At this resolution of the plot Paul has compromised his temptation to rival Morse—to marry Kate and write the book himself.
When he leaves the doctor's office, where he has disguised
himself as Bruce (the medical student) Halliday (successful
novelist), the doctor mentions that Paul will be going home
soon. Paul reacts:

Home. Paul's mind held its hands over the little brazier that
this word alone could light in his mind. Home. Where it didn't
matter whether you came back with the trophy or the scar.

But now he had no fear that it would be the scar. With this
man in league with him against his sickness, it would surely be
routed.

When Buckler turns home to the material of the first novel to
complete his cycle, similarly the disguises are dropped, and it
does not matter if the book (originally intended as "Fireflies
and Freedom") is the scar or the trophy. And when he turns
to an organizing principle for the "memoirs," his death (of
talent or otherwise) is not signalled like David's by the flight
of a single partridge. He realizes the multiple texture of style
that could be provided with the sufficient sense of continuity
found in a simple rhyme:

> one crow for sorrow
> two crows for joy
> three crows for a girl
> four crows for a boy
> five crows for silver
> six crows for gold
> seven crows a secret that can never be told . . .

Buckler might say that this introduction attempts to do for
The Cruelest Month what a parent might for his crippled child.
This is not the intention. It could be used as an essay to bridge
the gap—if, indeed, there is any gap—between Ian A. Atkinson's "Imagery and Symbolism" (which studies *The Mountain
and the Valley*) and John C. Orange's "On *Ox Bells and
Fireflies*." These two extracts from thesis studies provide the

conclusion to this volume of criticism by careful assimilation of the following material as it applies to the first and last books. They do not deal here with *The Cruelest Month*. The rationale of this introduction, therefore, is only latent and implicit in their conclusions. The very last word, however brief, may be found in Harry Brown's letter.

GREGORY M. COOK

Acadia University
October 26, 1970

MY FIRST NOVEL

ERNEST BUCKLER

What I happen to be is a farmer who writes, not a writer who
farms. That's why my novel had to be composed almost entirely
on second wind. It's physically impossible for me to assemble
two consecutive thoughts in the morning. Even if that were *not*
the time for milking, or mowing, or what not. Mornings, my
colons are really sluggish. If a leaky pig's trough didn't have
to be stuffed with birch bark—or it wasn't the day for the
brindle heifer's romance or something such—I tried to do a
little work on the book in the afternoons. But my life as a
writer really began after supper. Then, after a short pause for
braiding up my nerves with a little reading, I slugged it out with
the muse for exactly three hours. Perhaps, though, my most
productive periods were those in bed, when the darn thing kept
me awake.

I know it's sticking your neck out to say this novel was one
you *had* to write. Too many people are free to reply that they
find no such compulsion to read it. But—despite that risk—
mine was.

It certainly wasn't done for pleasure. If there is any purgatory more undiluted than attempting to trap the quicksilver of
life with the laggard spring of words, I don't know it. You so
often feel like those fatuous ancients who thought to enclose the
bird with a wall. For life is so infinitely tangential. It flees touch
like a ball of mercury flees the finger. And you find not its
smallest feature in clear-outline, but always in solution. And

"My First Novel," by Ernest Buckler. From an unpublished text prepared and read by the author for CBC Toronto (1953). By permission
of Ernest Buckler.

so dauntingly various. *War and Peace* is alleged to have said everything about everything. But it doesn't. Even if Tolstoy had included the yacht race he so flayed himself for omitting, it wouldn't have. The greatest novel ever written is a mere phrase, a word, a letter, if you like, in the infinite language of human relations.

How, then, can you precipitate even the tiniest crystal from this solution? Must you suspend some sort of string in it, as physicists do to precipitate salt crystals? And, if so, what string?

One writer's idea of how it's done is no better than another's. All are mere personal whim. But I think that the string you use is your characters. Know them thoroughly at the beginning, put them into the solution, and somehow the novel will accrete around them. I tried to get my characters straight right at the start—to know exactly where they were going to wind up— And then I let them more or less work their own passage. Although it wasn't quite as clinical as that sounds. Nothing was worked out altogether cold-bloodedly or singly. I think in those projects which you find really compelling, characters, theme, development, and, above all, the sort of—shall we say, "climate" of the thing?—come to you all together. In embryo, at least. The rest is largely nurture and photography.

I didn't fret too much about action. For myself, as soon as complications in a book start popping, I always feel like muttering to the characters: "Oh, for heaven's sake, stop scurrying around advancing the plot! Sit still a minute till we get a squint at your insides." For I think that insides are far more important . . . *and* interesting—than outsides. That action—despite the wired-upper-lip and prose-clipped-with-mat-scissors school—is far less important than its motivation. Nor did I ever wait on inspiration. I think that inspiration, by and large, is one great big myth. What really happens: you work and work toward an idea, and some sort of mold of the thing desired forms in your mind. Then—while you're chopping, or hoeing, or whatever—the subconscious gets going: fitting images against this mold, and when one of them—phrase, incident, or whatever—

slips into it, that tiny click you hear, that's what's mistaken for inspiration.

What I always *did* wait too long for, though, was a feeling of rightness about even the first draft. I had an incurable distaste for using, even temporarily, the stand-in phrase, the tentative line! And that can be crippling. Because nothing unlooses a chain of ideas like one, any one, already put down. An approximate idea can introduce you to just the one you want, as it is so often through your half-friends that you meet your whole ones. And it is so often curiously true that the only way you seem to arrive at the right spot is by the wrong path. Truth should be the *only* destination; but you should remember that the paths to it are expendable.

If there was anything else I learned, it was this: when you accomplish a bit that reads as if, brother, *that* must have been something hard to get expressed, don't stick your thumbs in your galluses and gloat. Spend another hour, or day, on it—until it sounds as if, hell, anyone could do that. You rarely achieve that happy effect, of course; because after rewriting *so* long, you can no longer tell if you're pruning fat or nerve. But it's a good target to aim at.

By the way, this novel—though it did try to show the texture of life in a village not altogether unlike the one I do know—and love—best, was not literally *autobiographical*. Except as all writing is—between the lines—autobiographical.

The six years the novel took, I spent in almost complete isolation. I've often been asked how much I minded being so out of contact with other writers. Well, it's wildly lonely, of course—especially when you have some little success you'd like to celebrate, with the only others who *can* know just what it means to you. But I had my mailbox. And the Godsent Diana Lockhart's travelling Bookmobile. Which brought me Elizabeth Bowen—who, incidentally, is the woman I love—E. M. Forster, Henry James, Dylan Thomas, Hemingway, Faulkner, Proust. In batches of twenty, sometimes.

And I think that isolation, however shriving personally, may be a good thing for a writer's work. My thoughts, anyway, are like mice. When the mind is quiet, they seem to pop out of their holes and scutter about much more freely than when I'm in company. I think, too, that when writers congregate in clutches, or coveys, or whatever the word is in that connection, they talk too much. They dissipate with their tongues what they should be funnelling through their pens. And when this talk is about work in progress, it takes the edge off the performance itself. Writer's shop talk isn't half as rewarding as people's, anyway. To cite the first instance that comes to mind: I once said to a country friend of mine—91 years old, and just starting to get the old age pension—I said, "What are you going to do with all your money?" He said, "I'm going to spend every damn cent of it on *women!*" He meant it too. Now where would you pick up anything like that in an atelier?

Another danger, I think, is that when writers associate too much with each other, a sort of inbreeding starts to develop. You half-hear them saying: Now we'll form a hermetically sealed little group, and the password will be Yoknapatawpha, or Anna Livia Plurabelle, or something, eh? And so on. Which is disastrous. And eventually they may come to write almost entirely about writing. Which is ruinous. At best, writing is only shadow. Writing about writing, then, is a dim second carbon indeed. On the other hand, you mustn't, except *while* you're writing, have lived entirely to yourself. Pure ivory tower stuff may be as miraculous and delicate as the silk a spider spins out of *his* own viscera—but it's equally thin. So thin that you could use it too for bombsights. But only for the most microscopic of targets.

Now comes the hard part. It's very difficult to mention the success of your own novel, without striking a note either of insufferable conceit or nauseating modesty. But simply as fact —mine has done all right. In the States, anyway. Promotion there, and critical response, were all anyone could ask for. And sales there, though not exactly astronomical, have been very good indeed. Critical reception in Canada has also been most heartening. But I'm afraid I can detect no brush-fire of popular enthusiasm. Again, this is fact, not winging: All the yachts you could build with your Canadian royalties you could sail in your bathtub.

And, of course, for every person here who welcomes the novel's frankness, there's another, who recoils from any mention of life's (which is to say, his own) basic impulse, as if it were a Lazarus Bell. Just the same, I think that Canadian writing is definitely breaking away from this crocheting of little tea-cosies of genteel prose for the excruciatingly prim—and is turning out stuff of real flesh, blood, bone, *and* spirit. Witness Bill Mitchell.

And it's also heartening to note that all this flapdoodle about the Canadian writer's first obligation being to write like a Canadian (however that is) is dying down. If you're a Canadian, and write as honestly as you can about what you know—here or anywhere else—and the result doesn't *sound* Canadian—well, no conscious attitude you strike will ever make it sound so. If you're a Canadian and want to write a distinctively Canadian novel, I'd say: just trust your natural processes, Mac, just trust your natural processes. Don't *try* to write *like* anything—except yourself. Again, witness Bill Mitchell.

So your first novel is finally done, such as it is. You look at the first bound copy, and you feel a mite like a lady who once said to me about the beautiful job a mortician had done on her late aunt: "I tell you, Ern," she said, "if I hadn'ta knowed her, I wouldn'ta knowed it was her!" The book's shape is so compact. If a novel were to bear any physical likeness to its genesis, it would look more like one of those tortuous deltas of the nervous system. You pick it up. The print has a kind of almost strident assurance. As if it were quite satisfied with itself, whereas you were never absolutely sure you were satisfied with any of it. And it looks so immaculately clean. You'd half-expected that the hours of indecision about that particular passage, writing in and then rubbing out in your brain, would somehow turn up as a smudge on the physical page. You'd half-expected that the countless half-entertained ideas you'd later discarded would show up as shadow. Where are all the ramifications that each period cut short? You'd half-expected to see them, trailing like fibrous bookmarks from each end. And where is the big white gap—which should represent that whole evening you sat there, but not one word came. On the credit side, the irreducible clumsiness of this passage seems somehow to have righted itself. But, alas, what's happened to the resonance of that one, which detonates now like a damp fuse? But there the book is. At least something tangible. (And, by the way, there'll be nothing like it to winnow your true friends from your false, one way or another.) Why, then, don't you feel the glee you'd always envisioned for this point? But you don't. You feel, instead, as hollow as a conch. As if you'd dipped yourself completely dry, and no more ideas would ever seep back in.

But eventually—after what George Moore called "the agony of being without a theme"—they do. And then you transfer your ambitions—much chastened, though—to the next book. And the first one takes on a little the character of some past indiscretion you'd half-prefer to forget.

Yes, you do tackle another. Knowing quite well that you're facing all over again another endless see-saw of those two almost equally agonizing days: the one when you feel that—if you could somehow circumvent that curious little block—it's just on the tip of your tongue to be Shakespeare. And the other, when you feel that the whole bloody works has been one big self-delusion: that what you were really cut out to be was an egg-candler.

Why do you do it, then? The answer, I guess, *is:* that if writing is hell, not writing is worse.

FIVE REVIEWS OF
THE MOUNTAIN AND THE VALLEY

1. GOOD EARTH, GOOD PEOPLE

STUART KEATE

Nothing much exciting happens on the Canaan farm in Nova Scotia's lovely Annapolis valley. Grandmother Ellen hooks rugs; father Joseph and his sons, Dave and Chris, kill pigs, move rocks, saw wood and go fishing; mother Martha does up preserves, papers a wall and puts a hot stick of wood in bed at night to warm her children's feet.

Their lives move ahead calmly, steadily, with a proud but quiet dignity. Ellen's patchwork rug links up past and present: a piece of Joseph's sweater (brown, for the earth); Martha's scarf (pink, for the sky); a patch from Christopher's Indian suit (green, for the stalk); a corner of the dress Anna wore, the day she went to work in Halifax (blue, for the flower).

Author Buckler's paean to the good earth and good people is told in terms of two decades in the life of David Canaan. A shy, introspective boy who dreams of acting and writing. David is disturbed by his bucolic surroundings, but he is so much a part of them that he cannot run away. In his last, moving hike to the mountaintop he looks down on the rich forests and fields and concludes: "It's perfect here."

If at times the narrative seems uneven and formless, the language a little overripe ("The pasture decayed gently, lingering after sentience, and lacquered after death with the wistful

"Good Earth, Good People," by Stuart Keate. In *The New York Times Book Review* 57 (October 26, 1952), p. 5. © 1952 by the New York Times Company. Reprinted by permission.

fall-stain. . . ."), the author imparts to it a haunting eloquence, an almost aching sensuality. In the field of psychological conflict —between son and father, and between adolescents tentatively exploring the mysteries of sex—Mr. Buckler's work is perceptive and altogether first-rate. His ear for the native dialect is unerring.

The Mountain and the Valley, a first novel, justifies much of the promise shown by Mr. Buckler as a prize-winning short story writer, both in Canada and the United States. Had his excesses of imagery, his infatuation with the language, been curbed by a somewhat sterner editorial pencil, it is altogether possible that this good book might have been a great one.

---

2.   EVERY LITTLE MOVEMENT HAS A MEANING ALL ITS OWN

WILLIAM ARTHUR DEACON

The smell of the tree grew suddenly and the memory of the smell of the oranges and the feel of the nuts. In that instant suddenly, ecstatically, burstingly, buoyantly, enclosingly, sharply, safely, stingingly, watchfully, batedly, mountingly, softly, ever so softly, it was Christmas Eve.

Younger intellectuals hereabouts may take heart because one Canadian's first novel is a true fruit of Freud and James Joyce's *Ulysses. The Mountain and the Valley* is beautifully written— each word chiselled with loving care. Symbolism is found everywhere. As in the old song: "Every thought and feeling by some gesture may be shown"; and Ernest Buckler spares no effort to explain "the thoughts that lie too deep for tears." He also gives to commonplaces of farm life—such as some newly dug potatoes—a wealth of refined meaning we should never have guessed they possessed.

"Every Little Movement Has a Meaning All Its Own" by William Arthur Deacon. In *The Globe and Mail,* Toronto (November 29, 1952). Reprinted by permission.

This is a poetic prose; and it is just possible that the author's real affinity lies with the more serious and less comprehensible of the newer poets. But he is practical enough to wish to be read, hence fiction and this book which is physically beautiful. Paper, type, design are all in perfect taste, while the R. M. Powers jacket is the loveliest specimen to appear in 1952.

Let there be no doubt about the fact that Ernest Buckler is an exquisite artist in words. If he were to write nothing else, this novel would long be treasured as an example of how to wring significance from the most trivial circumstance, the most careless word, the most fleeting emotion.

Sometimes when you hear a train whistle and everything turns quiet around you, like the way flowers lie on a grave after the mourners have all gone home, or sometimes in the fall when the hay is cut and it's moonlight and it seems as if everything is somewhere else. . . .

A leaf drifted down from the chestnut tree before the house, as if undecided after it had left the twig. . . . the day of the dug-potatoes lying in the dusty sunshine like fruit in a mist-thin wine: the day of the frost-starched grass and the still yellow smell of the sweet fern or the huckleberry or anything your foot crushed. . . .

Beautiful as the verbiage is, indicating a distinguished mind, the common reader may well weary of keeping his mind always at the stretch to pick up the countless nuances. For *The Mountain and the Valley* is at the furthest remove from what blurb writers call "an exciting, fast-paced story."

It is, on the contrary, a slow, intricate tale of youthful frustration. The boy David gets his matriculation at the age of 12, just as Mr. Buckler did. He knew that, some day, he would become famous by writing a brilliant book. The tragedy is that the brainy lad was far above the heavy, rough work of the farm, to which he was chained by circumstances through long, long years.

The Mountain and the Valley is essentially an interpretation of the ill-defined thoughts of the characters and the translation of their feelings, often so tenuous that they, themselves, do not understand them. It is literary psychoanalysis and physical dissection.

Death is the most positive and frequent event in the narrative. Apart from the sheer magic of the old-fashioned Christmas, with which the story opens, the mood is consistently sombre. Two men drown, a young girl dies of cancer, the father is killed by a falling tree and so on.

At the end, the mature David is living on the valley farm, symbolic of the hated, workaday grind, and alone save for his ancient grandmother, who has lost her mind. He ascends to the top of the mountain—representing vision, achievement and power—and there experiences a transmutation into bliss. This reviewer is, unfortunately, unable to decide whether the illumination on the mount implies the final healing of David's soul, or whether his brain has at last parted company with mundane reality, or whether he has died of heart failure and we are dealing with a disincarnate intelligence. The fact that the grandmother has, at last, and at the same moment, finished weaving the rug, probably indicates David's death. If so, we are glad that he died happy.

---

3. FINE FARM LIFE STUDY

S. MORGAN-POWELL

There are very few Canadian novels dealing with farm life. This is the more surprising in view of the fact that the farming population of Canada is about sixteen per cent of the total population of this country. It may be that farm life is not a subject that appeals to the average Canadian; whether it would appeal to the average Canadian farmer, as such, I am not in the position to say. The fact remains that farmers and their way of living have very seldom intrigued the attention of any of our leading authors.

From "The Bookshelf," by S. Morgan-Powell. In *The Montreal Star* (December 20, 1952). Reprinted by permission.

The Mountain and the Valley, a first novel which tells a story of a farming family in the Annapolis Valley of Nova Scotia, is therefore all the more welcome. The author, *Ernest Buckler,* is the son of a farmer, was brought up on a farm, and has run his own farm for the past twelve years during which his contacts with the outside world have been few and far between. Mr. Buckler tells us that "an author's problems get scant sympathy in the country. Writing is regarded as at most a harmless eccentricity, like an abnormal appetite for marsh greens. Besides, farming and writing don't mix too well. But farming is a good free way of life."

If we may judge from the outcome of mixing farming and writing in Mr. Buckler's case, then I fancy most people who read *The Mountain and the Valley* will hope that he will continue to write and go on living on a farm, which he apparently does for his health.

Mr. Buckler tells the story of the little farming community of Entremont and particularly of the Canaan family, which consists of Grandmother Ellen, her son Joseph and his wife Martha, his two sons, Chris and David, and his daughter Anna. David is the hero of the tale, which covers his life from child-hood until he is thirty.

David as a boy was both sensitive and shy. Many farmers' sons are, and very often those qualities make them seem of a dull or retiring disposition. The Canaan Family lived a life very close to the soil. Joseph was a man of reserve but of deep feelings. He loved his wife and children and his affection for them was far deeper than mere words. He was respected and liked by the whole community; his wife loved him deeply and his children were quietly proud of him. Chris, the older boy, was growing up a man of the farm, but David was divided in his affection. There were certain things about farm life that he did not like: its crudities and the roughness of many of its contacts. But the sensitivity of his nature enabled him to appreciate the outdoor life, the constant change in the landscape as the seasons passed unhurrying by, the beauty of nature in her varying moods. Mr. Buckler is himself a man whose eyes and ears are attuned to nature's harmonies, and he reveals this in his description of farm life both in the open and within the quietude of home. He can make a landscape glow in the mind's eye of his reader and just as easily and arrestingly endow a kitchen scene with life.

. . . .

The drama in *The Mountain and the Valley* moves steadily just as normal farm life does. The interest in this book lies more in its character portrayals and in the strikingly realistic analyses of emotions. Mr. Buckler has a skill in vivid imagery that must be ranked as remarkable in Canadian fiction. But he also understands the working of the adolescent mind in youths and girls, and his analyses in this connection are stamped with sympathy, deep understanding, and compassion. David was a boy who had a great capacity for affection; in fact, the whole Canaan family were bound together by love. The sentiments of affection which linked them also enabled them to understand each other, and, when understanding was not easy, to keep silence yet to convey their understanding of a desire for isolation at times.

Mr. Buckler has a passion for detail, and this inclines him at times to a realistic over-elaboration which may not appeal to purists, but there can never be the slightest doubt as to his sincerity.

One feels that his portraiture is based upon experience. He seems to understand his characters, yet there is never any suggestion of a built-up portrait. The human touch is unfailing and at times very moving.

There is much beautiful writing in this book. There are also painful passages of bitter realism. Mr. Buckler does not seek to gild farm life as something wholly free from the disillusions that the city holds. He has been a farmer for twelve years and lived on a farm for much longer than that, and he can take the long view. There is no special pleading here. He presents the picture as a whole, with its virtues and its defects, the qualities that make farm life worth living and those that cannot be grasped on first contact in their real significance or their inevitability. The reader will understand why David could never bring himself to face a lifetime on the farm with equanimity. There must be many farmers' sons like him, just as there are many who, having grown up with the soil, feel that it has its advantages and its attractions, as well as features recurrent and inevitable which must be dealt with but need not be dwelt upon to the exclusion of those things worth while.

To David's father and his mother, and to his brother, farming was a vocation. It is the men who regard farming in this way who are the backbone of the farming industry upon which this Dominion has been founded and developed.

Mr. Buckler has done a fine work in *The Mountain and the Valley.* I regard this as one of the most significant novels by a Canadian that has been published for many years. There are traces here and there of the inexperienced hand, lack of reticence now and then, and lack of restraint also; but he must have recognized these faults, and in his future work, to which I for one shall look forward with keen anticipation, it is reasonable to assume they will no longer appear.

So long as the country can breed writers of Mr. Buckler's calibre and human understanding, the outlook for the development of Canadian literature that will count for something more than trivial reading entertainment is encouraging.

---

4. A STUDY OF HUMAN RELATIONS

CLAUDE BISSELL

. . . .

Ethel Wilson's two novelettes are accomplished and delightful, but they are not major works. She has still to demonstrate her

From "Letters in Canada: 1952—Fiction," by Claude Bissell. In *The University of Toronto Quarterly* 22 (April 1953), pp. 290-92. By permission of Claude Bissell.

power to sustain a full-length novel (*Hetty Dorval* was, after all, little more than a novelette, and *The Innocent Traveller* was fragmentary and discursive). Ernest Buckler's *The Mountain and the Valley* . . . , on the other hand, is, in my opinion, a major work: a full-length novel in which a single intense vision welds the parts into a whole.

It may be argued that technically Mr. Buckler's success is achieved on a comparatively simple level. This is a novel of education and, like most novels of this kind, it is, one suspects, strongly autobiographical. The form of the novel of education is predetermined; the character of the protagonist and the course of the action are as rigidly prescribed as they are in a fairy-tale. The hero must be sensitive, at odds with his immediate environment, finally pushed to active rebellion. The novel must proceed chronologically in an orderly progression from childhood to adulthood. Up to a point Mr. Buckler follows the prescription. We accompany his hero, David Canaan, younger son of a farming family in Nova Scotia, from early boyhood to death. Buckler picks out clusters of events that occur at various stages in David's development and works them into separate sections, arranged chronologically. But—and this constitutes Mr. Buckler's originality—he manages to triumph over the tyranny of linear time. The introduction of a prologue and an epilogue, each of which deals with the final day in the life of the hero, is a device that helps to break down the simple, temporal sequence. But what is far more effective is the use that Buckler makes of the character of the grandmother. She is, as it were, a still point in the jumble of events, a sort of eternal present who ranges back and forth in memory so that past and present become to her, and then to the reader, almost indistinguishable. She is constantly weaving a rug from clothes long since discarded by members of the family. And this rug, with its multiple strands and its associations with past events and people, becomes a symbol of the power of human relations to withstand the gnawing of time.

If Mr. Buckler escapes from the simple chronological type of narrative in novels of education, he escapes also from the usual psychological pattern. Up to a point the resemblances to the pattern are strong. His hero is sensitive and precocious. He is also an artist struggling in his obscure way to forge in the smithy of his soul the uncreated conscience of his race. He becomes obsessed with the need to capture in words the exact shade of feeling and emotion. His family lies beyond the world of imagination and feeling in which he has his being. His father and mother and his older brother are hopelessly wedded to ancestral ways and to the crude, monotonously repeated phrases that serve among them for human communication. The community, moreover, is primitive and unprogressive, and David can find no strong allies among his daily associates. Here, then, is the familiar conflict that we find in a score of novels about the spiritual growth of sensitive young men. Here is the human bondage in which the hero finds himself, and which, in the concluding chapters, he triumphantly casts off. But Buckler, although he gives to David his moments of passionate rebellion, is not interested in such a simple, dramatic reversal. He is in search of a subtler conflict.

The Mountain and the Valley is a study of human relations as they work themselves out in a family, separated by deep personal differences and yet united by love and affection. Joseph, the father, is a man of simple integrity and kindness. Between him and his wife, Martha, there is an understanding no less strong for being unexpressed. With them "speech broke rather than forged the quiet contact." The older son, Chris, is a replica of his father: strong, forthright, and inarticulate. David is, of course, the member of the family set apart, as is, in a lesser way, his twin sister Anna, shy and pretty, to whom David is peculiarly attached. David's parents and older brother, puzzled by and even resentful of his finer speech and thoughts, nevertheless see in him a being greater than themselves. His intellectual eminence becomes to them a source of family pride. Buckler, then, is not proclaiming, as so many novelists of this century have done, the sacred necessity for rebellion, nor is he making an austere religion of human isolation. This is a study in the power of the group, in the way in which human beings, living in separate worlds, are yet made one with each other. This is not to say that *The Mountain and the Valley* is a novel about idyllic, rural life. Buckler knows that human affection and love are delicately poised, and that if the balance is disturbed they explode with violence and tragedy. This is what happens in *The Mountain and the Valley,* and it is told with a realism that, by the standards of the Canadian novel, is fierce and unrelenting.

This is a novel that is written with intensity and with painstaking care. Like his hero, Buckler has tried to say things exactly. He is striving to avoid the generalized phrase, the easy cliché, the long and sonorous sentence, and to make each word a servant of his vision. At times there is straining and pretentiousness, and there is certainly little humour. It is a measure of Buckler's strength that he cannot easily be fitted into any of the usual critical categories. For felicity in natural description and in the depiction of rural life one thinks of W. O. Mitchell's *Who Has Seen the Wind.* (Incidentally, Mitchell is one of a group to whom Buckler dedicates his book.) For intensity in the analysis of feeling and of thought one thinks of Sinclair Ross's *As For Me and My House* or one or two of Morley Callaghan's novels. But speculations like these are merely a literary game. What is important is that *The Mountain and the Valley* is a fine Canadian novel, in many respects the best that has been written in this country. One hopes that this is the first of many novels that Ernest Buckler will write.

Novelists like Ethel Wilson and Ernest Buckler have no need to wave flags or to wrap themselves up in the heavy robes of history. Their novels spring out of an intense realization of a human predicament, and everything else grows naturally and inevitably from that. One notices that neither Miss Wilson nor Mr. Buckler spends time erecting a framework of reference. We do not find pages about the historical and social background of Vancouver and the Nova Scotia valleys. They take their Canadian material for granted and then proceed to talk about the streets of Vancouver and the countryside of Nova Scotia as if they were, as indeed they are, rich material for the creative artist. There is nothing self-conscious and assertive about their use of the local scene. They happen to know Vancouver and Nova Scotia and the people who live there; and this constitutes for them sufficient reason for writing about them. What I find distressing is that this commanding use of Canadian material has not been able to give either writer a national reading public. Ethel Wilson, I suspect, is widely read in British Columbia but does not penetrate seriously the bestseller lists of Toronto. Buckler has been enthusiastically received in the United States, but I am not aware of any reception, cordial or otherwise, that he has been given in his own country. The great threat to our cultural life is not that it will be swamped by an uncritical nationalism, but that it will dwindle into little, stagnant pools of provincialism.

---

5. A STUDY OF THE HUMAN SPIRIT

KATHERINE DOUGLAS

The publication of a first novel by this remarkable Nova Scotian writer will be greeted as an event by those who have already encountered his all too frequent short stories and articles.

It may well be that the purists will not accept *The Mountain and the Valley* as being a novel in the accepted classical sense, since there is little or no "action" or "plot" and little character development, the characters seeming to have signifcance primarily in their impact on the central character, David. *The Mountain and the Valley* is an account, then, of the reactions of an exceptional child and man to the life he finds around him on an Annapolis Valley farm.

We follow the sensitive David through the ecstasies and agonies of boyhood, sharing his revulsion at the crudities of farm life and understanding his delight in the deeply satisfying things that go with country living. As David grows from child-

From a review of *the Mountain and the Valley* by Katherine Douglas. In *The Dalhousie Review* 32 (Winter 1953), pp. iii, v. By permission of Katherine Douglas.

hood to adolescence, there is an increasing awareness that he is somehow different from the others. And, though he loves his farm home and his family passionately, the love is mixed with a longing for things beyond. Torn between these two loyalties, there comes a day when he faces the knowledge that he can neither go nor stay.

The foregoing might be an outline of any one of a dozen present-day novels dealing with the lives of farm people, their joys and sorrows. But this book goes much deeper—it is a powerful study of the human spirit.

The middle part of the novel does not quite fulfill the promise of the earlier part: there is little indication of what David's life has been between the period of late adolescence and early middle age. Perhaps this is intentional on the author's part. At any rate it does not seem to detract from the effectiveness of the latter part, which moves swiftly to an almost unbearable climax.

Here the author describes David's contemplation of what his life has become—his inevitable isolation which is his only refuge and at the same time his supreme torture. Here we are shown the bare bones of thought process, not in the abstract way of the stream-of-consciousness writer, but with the clinical skill of a biologist dissecting a frog. For example:

But just as I move on to something else, the thought breaks down like a stream forking in the sand. Then the forks fork. Then the forks' forks fork, like the chickenwire pattern of atoms. . . .

And again:

He could think of anything now. Everything seemed to be an aspect of something else. There seemed to be a thread of similarity running through the whole world. A shape could be like a sound; a feeling like a shape; a smell the shadow of a touch— His senses seemed to run together.

Ernest Buckler's supreme gift seems to be his unerring use of words to evoke half-forgotten but instantly recognized pictures, odors, feelings, thoughts and impressions. He bends and shapes his words with such startling originality and power that the reader may find himself half wishing that the writer would restrain himself. This reader was constantly reminded, while reading *The Mountain and the Valley,* of the mingled simplicity and intensity found in the paintings of Van Gogh. And indeed, Ernest Buckler is a painter, using words instead of colors.

This is David as a little boy on Christmas Eve:

He opened the bag of nuts and rolled one in his palm, then put it back. He put his hand deep down into the bag and rolled all the nuts through his fingers . . . the crinkled walnuts with the lung-shaped kernels . . . . . [sic] then he leaned over and smelled the bag of oranges . . . . . [sic] the sharp sweet, reminding, fulfilling smell of the oranges [that] was so incarnate of to-morrow . . . .

In this year of alleged grace, 1952, when the taste of the general reading public appears to have reached a peak in appetite for inanity and mediocrity, not to mention depravity, it will be interesting to note the reaction to this newest Canadain novel. For those who will read it and can understand it, *The Mountain and the Valley* offers a moving and rewarding experience, and there can be no doubt that its author has made a valuable contribution to North American literature.

THE MOUNTAIN AND THE VALLEY

R. E. WATTERS

. . . .

This ultimate question of the purpose of living, the essential values of human experience, the attempt to detect a meaningful pattern in a human existence, is very near the centre of the first and so far only novel written by the third Canadian novelist on our bill-of-fare for this evening. I could safely assume that everyone here had either *read* something by MacLennan or de la Roche—or, at the very least, had *heard* the names of these two authors. But it is all too likely that this third novelist and his book are unknown to almost all of you, even though it was published two years ago. I hope I am wrong in this, since I would like to believe that Ernest Buckler and his novel, *The Mountain and the Valley,* are better known than I fear to be the case.

Ernest Buckler is a native of Nova Scotia—a man in his forties—who has been living on a farm in the Annapolis Valley for more than a dozen years. He has published a number of short stories and articles, but he writes slowly and, it is said, spent five to six years on *The Mountain and the Valley* (1952). Those years, however, were very profitably spent for Canadian literature. There has never been a "first novel" written in Canada as excellent as this one.

Now this is a very large claim—one that should be supported by adequate illustration and evidence; and I could easily have devoted all my time here tonight to this single book. But since I hope each of you will soon be spending at least one entire evening reading this book, I shall content myself with only a few general points and a minimum of evidence.

From a public lecture, entitled "Three Canadian Novelists," given in Victoria, B.C., in the fall of 1954 and again in Nanaimo, B.C., in February 1955. By permission of R. E. Watters.

First a word about the narrative structure of this novel to suggest one reason for the novel's significance. *The Mountain and the Valley* is a novel of growth or development, in which we trace the expanding experience of the principal character passing from childhood to maturity—a common enough subject, and one usually presented in a straightforward linear succession of chronological episodes—beads of incident on a string of character. But Buckler is, quite rightly, dissatisfied with this technique in that it oversimplifies the complex fabric of human life; in consequence, he employs two devices which very effectively enrich and deepen the presentation.

The first of these devices is his use of a prologue and an epilogue, both dealing with the last day in the life of David Canaan, the principal character. The epilogue which concludes the book continues immediately from where the prologue at the begining has left off. Clearly suggested here is the truth that every moment of our lives is the cumulative total of every preceding moment, and that we are what we are because of what we were—what we saw, heard, felt, and thought in all our yesterdays. Between the prologue and the epilogue we experience, with David, the living texture of his yesterdays, before we continue with him his last day of life and he begins his climb to the top of his mountain, to meet his death in the dust of a snow-flurry. This splitting of the last day is, I can assure you, extraordinarily effective workmanship, perfectly employed to fit the theme of the book.

The second, and still more successful, narrative device employed by Buckler is his use of a rug-making grandmother. We meet her in the prologue tearing up discarded clothes into the rags she needs for the simple-patterned rug she is creating, and we meet her on all of David's yesterdays, weaving a similar rug —or maybe the same rug—like a deity in an ancient myth bending over the web of time. As she rips and braids her rags and scraps, she recalls—sometimes clearly, often confusedly— the persons or incidents connected with these mute tokens of a vanished past time. She destroys the leavings of the past in order to incorporate them into the pattern of the present. The grandmother endures through time like a living embodiment of the past in the present. She is nevertheless a symbol also of the eternal present whose function is always the interweaving of our yesterdays with our todays in some kind of useful and meaningful pattern. The comic and the tragic moments from the past are brought together in new interrelationships, just as a scrap from the blue blanket, that received David and his twin sister at birth, is juxtaposed with a strip from the new shirt the father wore on the day he was killed, and with a piece from a homespun stocking cap spun and dyed by the grandmother and worn by Chris the day he was taken to the woods for the first time.

I don't wish to give the impression—as I may have done—that this symbolic rug-weaving dominates the book. It doesn't. Its function is that of the canvas base into which the coloured scraps of experience are woven. One detects the symbol at the edges, so to speak, or between patches of bright colour—and one knows it is there and must be there—but it does not greatly attract an observer's attention unless he is describing, as I am here doing, just how the rug of David's life history is constructed.

The general design of this life history is simple, and it is, in a broad way, suggested by the very title, *The Mountain and the Valley*. David Canaan is an exceptionally gifted child rising out of an ordinary farm community, as the mountain rises out of the valley. His family, like his neighbours, are limited in their mental and spiritual horizons; they are absorbed in ancestral habits of action, thought, and speech, and are quite content to live below the peaks of self-awareness. They live and speak the clichés of experience and expression, with no desire to climb above the daily routine formulas and to see freshly and accurately, or express themselves precisely and intelligibly. To them, "A tree was a tree, a thing for the ax. A field was a field. You hauled across it when it was frozen, plowed it when it was soft. That's all there was to it." Their minds contained the *ingredients* of thought, but those ingredients slithered and mixed in their minds without really *shaping* themselves into single or clear thoughts at all. It is not a matter of illiteracy or faulty education, however—it is an attitude towards life, the acceptance of the ready-made response, the stereotyped reaction, the dullness of expression, which is not *always* synonymous with dull *feeling*. David comes to understand this and to understand them; he can employ their little formulas and reactions, even supply them with the kind of pat response they crave—but they can take in only as much of him as their horizon's boundary. From the valley floor only one face of the mountain is visible, but from the mountain the entire valley is exposed to view, with all its worn paths and hidden recesses.

As he grows older, David is increasingly obsessed with the desire and need to experience life in its sharp intensity and to capture in some manageable form—for example, in words— the exact sensation, the precise shade of feeling or pitch of emotion. Emotionally he is strongly bound to his family, but he is gradually isolated, spiritually and intellectually, except when he descends to their level; for in a general way the family is at one with their neighbours. To them, words are for blunt, practical purposes only—subtleties in language or in any other form of expression, for either pleasure or keener appreciation, are quite beyond them. We are told—and this is quite characteristic—that speech breaks rather than forges the love that links the father and the mother. Notice the incident when David quarrels with the father, talks "high" to him, and runs off — meets some city people in a car and uses his educated language *with* them—and compares it with how he used such terms *against* his father.

I hope I'm not making it seem that David is nothing but an intellectual snob or that his life in family and community was one unrelieved agony. The truth is otherwise. David is not the "sensitive boy" in a crude environment that we often encounter in literature. On the contrary, to many readers David —particularly in his boyhood—may seem all too crude himself in his pleasures and experiences and thoughts—for this book has been accused of being full of "barnyard bawdiness." David is sensitive, all right, but his sensitivity differs from the rather weak softness, the "easily hurt" emotionalism, that so often comes to mind when the word "sensitive" is used. Physically and emotionally David appears rugged, if not "tough"—though some of this "toughness" is an armour he wears. But in another manner entirely, he is indeed sensitive. He is sensitive because his senses are keen in a community where sensory response is blunted by utility and erased by custom. He is sensitive because he is intellectually discriminating—capable of keen analysis of thought, aware of subtleties of feeling and human interrelationships—and capable, too, of exact expression of those thoughts, feeling and relationships.

Since childhood David had known himself to be different in degree from his companions and family and, although Buckler as narrator shows this difference from the beginning, David himself does not fully understand or appreciate it till much later. He begins to discover what he is, about the time he is recovering from a bad fall from a rafter in the barn—a fall that left a scar on his character as well as his face, and left a permanent ache in his head. I cannot do better than read a few sentences from the novel itself:

It was a book Dr. Engles had sent him. It was different from any book he'd ever read. It was supposed to be a good book; but at first it seemed dusty, like something old.

And then his eyes fell on one sentence: "He turned back to the empty house and his heart bent forward against a wind." He caught his breath. That's exactly the way *he'd* felt when anyone had gone away.

Then there was: "A shaft of memory stabbed him like the slash of a branch against a window pane in the night . . . ," "the sound of crickets winding their watches . . . ," "Lint made a knitting pattern in the interstices of the screen," "It was that shocking cry of a child in extreme pain, which you mistake at first for laughing . . ." He had the flooding shock of hearing things stated exactly for the first time.

Suddenly he knew how to surmount everything. That loneliness he'd always had—it got forgotten, maybe, weeded over— but none of it had ever been conquered. (And all that time the key to freedom had been lying in these lines, this book.) There was only one way to possess anything: to *say* it exactly. Then it would be outside you, captured and conquered.

This discovery of the potentialities of language leads him to a frantic effort to pursue things relentlessly to their essence and to search for an underlying meaning to experience—an effort that often ends in frustration, to be sure.

[He felt he] could think of anything now. Everything seemed to be an aspect of something else. There seemed to be a thread of similarity running through the whole world. A shape could be like a sound; a feeling like a shape, a smell the shadow of a touch—His senses seemed to run together.

And yet as David himself had to admit:

. . . just as I move on to something else, the thought breaks down like a stream forking in the sand. Then the forks fork. Then the forks' forks fork, like the chicken-wire pattern of atoms.

It is not until the very end of the book that David finally discovers what his relationship to his family and fellow men *ought* to be. As he races up the wintry mountainside despite a strained heart, passing the scenes of pleasurable and painful incidents from his yesterdays, he wins through to a revelation that he need not live a lonely life, frustrating to himself and worthless to others—he need not be isolated from his fellows because of his unique interests or gifts. But, instead, he can find a means of communion and fellowship with them. The mountain is not without use to the valley—indeed, without the one, the other would not be what it is. David can be a means of expression for his people, a voice giving utterance to what they cannot utter for themselves—and can do so not for his own ego's gratification, but in order to release in them qualities they themselves do not now know they possess.

David's hoped-for function is, of course, essentially that of the master artist—the poet, dramatist, musician—the novelist of national character, the novelist of universal humanity.

Here is a brief passage from within a few pages of the end of the book:

(Once, while he was still in school, he had composed a petition from all the men in the village, asking the government for a daily meal. When he read it back to them they heard the voice of their own reason speaking exactly in his. Their warm wonder at his little miracle of finding the words for it that they themselves couldn't find, or recognize for the words of their own thoughts until they heard him speak them, made him and them so fluid together that it worked in him like a kind of tears.)

As he thought of telling these things exactly, all the voices came close about him. They weren't swarming now. He went out into them until there was no inside left. He saw at last how you could *become* the thing you told.

It wouldn't be necessary to take them one by one. That's where he'd been wrong. All he'd have to do—oh, it was so gloriously simple—was to find their single core of meaning. It was manifest not differently but only in different aspects, in them all. That would be enough. A single beam of light is enough to light all the shadows, by turning it from one to another.

For a writer who is resolved to see life clearly and closely, and express it accurately, the hardest thing, in Hemingway's words, is "to survive and get his work done." The processes of learning the hard way have used up David's short span of life. But although David dies without getting his work done, Ernest Buckler, his creator, still lives. And Buckler's relationship to us can be that which David never lived to achieve for his people. We can welcome Buckler down from his mount of isolation—receive him gladly as a spokesman for the rest of us in the valley of all Canada—let him reveal to us and express for us things about our human nature and our world that we surely need to know.

I am rather fearful that by this hurried account of a very fine novel I may have given the impression that it is all philosophy and psychology, and not a community of human beings with character dramatized through speech and action—as good novels should be. The truth is, that it is only after subsequent reflection, stimulated of course by the great imaginative power of the narrative, that the philosophical pattern emerges. Reading the book is like living with the people in the valley—one is immersed in the succession of experiences and feelings in a way impossible to illustrate in a lecture. When one puts down the book one can climb out of the valley and look back to see the overall patterns worn by the feet that moved about down below. Then, as David came to see for himself, one can return to the valley's ways with new understanding and new perceptions.

I have said nothing about Buckler's prose style—but that you must taste for yourself. The startling originality and richness of Buckler's figurative language is quite without rival in Canada and probably elsewhere. I unreservedly recommend Buckler, with only one regret: that you can't have a second helping, since so far he has produced only this novel.

UNKNOWN LITERATURE

R. E. WATTERS

"No one knows my country, neither the stranger nor its own sons." So Bruce Hutchison asserts in *The Unknown Country.* Other missionaries have preceded and followed him. In the depths of the depression, William Arthur Deacon's *My Vision of Canada* flashed its message, rebuking the faint-hearted who were ignoring the physical and spiritual wealth all around them. Lately, such enthusiastic books as Roberts's *The Golden Hinge* and LeBourdais's *Canada's Century* have again been preaching energetically the alluring gospel of our golden century. Simultaneously, volumes like Harrington's *Northern Exposure* and Bolus's *Image of Canada,* full of breath-taking photographs of Canada's face and fortune, have been providing pictures that dazzle the benighted Canadian.

But in this Land of Promise, what about the human beings? What goes on in the hearts and minds of those who conquer the continent, harness the torrents, reap the harvests, erect the skyscrapers? Is the inner life behind the pictured faces—like the geography, the history, the statistics—an unknown country? If so, who will enlighten our inward darkness?

For every better known country a national literature has satisfactorily formulated and expressed the national character—*refining,* shaping, and uttering the essentials of the nation's spirit. Novelists, dramatists, poets create the human beings and the folk heroes in whom, as in a mirror, a people see for themselves what they are and what they wish to be. Have Canadian authors performed this service for Canadians?

In the *Report* of the Massey Commission some years ago,

"Unknown Literature," by R. E. Watters. In *Saturday Night* 70 (September 17, 1955), 31-33, 35-36. By permission of R. E. Watters.

Professor E. A. McCourt is quoted as saying: "The unpalatable truth is that today there exists no body of creative writing which reflects adequately, or with more than limited insight, the nature of the Canadian people and the historic forces which have made them what they are." Also quoted is an unnamed "prominent publisher": "The real failure must still rest with the failure to date of any large group of Canadian authors to express this country to the Canadian people in any really arresting way." Similar opinions are widespread, and contain truth; but not the whole truth.

Actually, our authors have done much better work than many of their compatriots will admit. Their task is a most formidable one. The Canadian national character is highly complex—a muddle of illogicalities, historical accidents and unassimilated influences. Our lack of a national flag hints at the larger problems. If as a nation we can't decide what few abstract qualities our flag should represent, it ill behooves us to rebuke our authors, who are grappling with an infinitely more complex subject, the Canadian human being.

To be sure, we Canadians don't get the literature we deserve. In truth, we get a literature much better than we deserve. What have we done to earn a great national literature? It may be true that literature, like rain, falls on the unjust as well as the just; but *great* literature, like a shower of manna, descends only upon a deserving people. Is it reasonable of us to demand Shakespeares when we aren't the kind of people the Elizabethans were: intensely patriotic, passionate in daily life, venturesome in literary tastes? To harvest an *Othello,* the Elizabethan playgoer cultivated how many lesser plays and playwrights? To reap a Henry James or a Hemingway, the American public tilled how many forgotten fields? Why should we Canadians demand a masterpiece in every little hill we hoe?

But that is not the limit of our demands. The first sprout in every hill must be a prize specimen, or we switch off the sprinkler. Yet the first plays even by Shakespeare, the first stories by Hawthorne, the first poems by most great poets, were 'prentice work.

Canadian authors are seldom permitted to unfurl all their leaves, let alone mature their fruit, in our cold climate. Our literature is strewn with a quite disproportionate number of one-book authors. Among novelists, for instance, consider such talented starters as these: Sinclair Ross, *As For Me and My House* (1941); Judith Cape (P. K. Page), *The Sun and the Moon* (1944); Selwyn Dewdney, *Wind Without Rain* (1946); Joyce Marshall, *Presently Tomorrow* (1946); James Benson Nablo, *The Long November* (1946); Christine van der Mark, *In Due Season* (1947); Henry Kreisel, *The Rich Man* (1948); Len Petersen, *The Chipmunk* (1949); Ernest Buckler, *The Mountain and the Valley* (1952).

We may still hope for another work from this last novelist, but I list Buckler's novel here to illustrate our attitude and our peril. The novel was published, like nearly half the others, by an American, not a Canadian, publisher. Last fall, when I tried to buy a copy from the Canadian agent of the American firm, I was informed that the book was out of print. (This doesn't mean that all copies printed had been sold—because within the past month or two I noticed the novel among books being "remaindered," at a cut price and without remuneration to the author.) The number of copies distributed in Canada and the amount of domestic promotion given to this new and remarkable talent may perhaps be indicated by this fact— that among scores of persons sufficiently interested in Canadian literature to attend lectures in the subject, only three or four had ever heard of this excellent novel. Last winter the novel was reprinted in a Signet Library paperback, but the returns to the author from such publication are often trivial. In all, the encouragement given Mr. Buckler to continue, and the financial means to support another long period of writing, must both have been slight. Yet *The Mountain and the Valley* is in my opinion the most distinguished and promising first novel ever published by any Canadian anywhere.

Furthermore, it is superior to the first books of most of the younger American and British novelists whose names are widely publicized in this country and whose work is known and read here. The contention that our literature is "really pretty poor stuff" is most frequently made by those who would salve their consciences for seldom reading our authors.

If Canadian readers spent all their time with the masterpieces of world literature no one could complain; but we do not. The standard of nothing-but-genius operates only against the native product. Moreover, all too often a well-intentioned reader learns about the good Canadian books only after their small printings are exhausted, or remaindered—and nearly all our friends are talking about the latest import anyway. The book journals and literary reviews, none of them published in Canada, inform us of current and available foreign books, and we choose our reading accordingly.

The same facts apply to Canadian poetry, though little of it is published by outside publishers. Not only have we too many one-book poets; even our "established" names are confined to two or perhaps three thin volumes. The result may be very choice poetry, but the display of some range and sustained productivity is almost indispensable for a great reputation. Canadian poets are seldom allowed more than one hundred pages or so, in total; usually much less.

I do not mean to suggest that quantity measures quality or that all of our one-book authors were necessarily rising geniuses blighted by the cold air of national indifference. Quite probably some were capable of only the single brief flight— and possibly one or two may yet accomplish a second. Elsewhere one might take comfort in a faith that good writing will always find a publisher and a public—but not in Canada.

A further curious characteristic of Canadians is our eagerness to relinquish national claim to the authors we have. I have been seriously asked, more than once, why I considered Stephen Leacock a Canadian humorist, since he was actually born in England. The sixty-eight years he lived in Canada apparently couldn't over-balance the seven years of his British boyhood. Yet the same persons would insist that the first thirty years in Canada of Gilbert Parker or Sara Jeannette Duncan are insufficient to color their later work abroad. Malcolm Lowry cannot be claimed, "of course," since he has spent only about fifteen years among us. On the other hand, some Canadians reject Mazo de la Roche as a native novelist simply because they consider her characters "too British" to be real Canadians.

Other peoples do not disown their talent so capriciously. Henry James and T. S. Eliot are claimed as major American authors despite their long residence abroad and adopted British citizenship. Even Ernest Hemingway, though retaining his citizenship, has lived most of his years abroad and has written chiefly about non-Americans. Similarly, the British have not relinquished Aldous Huxley or W. H. Auden or many others, whatever their residence or citizenship, and of course never hesitated about claiming as their own Joseph Conrad, of Poland.

If Canada doesn't value her Leacock's, others do. Writers on British humour embrace him—and so do Americans. A recent doctoral dissertation at an American university, for instance, bore the title: "Stephen Leacock, American Humorist". The same welcome is given Thomas Chandler Haliburton. Both Carman and Roberts are found in lists of American poets, and Callaghan and de la Roche among their writers of fiction. It is not only our natural resources that our neighbours are willing to expropriate.

Probably most good Canadian writing has been produced in the last two generations but no one can be quite sure of this, since bibliographical exploration of our past is wretchedly inadequate. I speak of our printed resources; what early manuscript material might be unearthed is almost totally unknown. The vigorous writing of our original United Empire Loyalists has rarely been examined and never collected in print in Canada. The Americans have done far more for these "enemies" than we have for our "patriots." There has never been a complete collection of the fugitive writings of Joseph Howe, one of our very few men of letters in politics.

The last volume of selections from Haliburton was compiled over thirty years ago; his complete works are almost unobtainable. Only about a fourth of George Frederick Cameron's poetry has ever been published—and the published fourth has been

out of print for over fifty years. And so it goes. Even in our
own day, probably less than half the output of our two best
playwrights (Robertson Davies and Lister Sinclair) has yet
appeared in print. What can Canadians know of their literature
past or present when so much of the evidence is absent? A great
literature comes to no nation which ignores its dead authors
and stints its living.

It should, indeed, surprise us that Canada has a literature at
all—but we have become complacent about inheriting un-
earned riches. Not so long ago the Laurentian shield was regarded as a valueless waste, and the Northlands were only the
barren lands. Then a few venturesome prospectors and pioneers
strengthened by faith and financed by a few investors (sometimes foreign, at that) demonstrated otherwise. The wealth was
really there—but not, to be sure, for the mere asking. To un-
cover and develop Canada's literary resources likewise demands
faith, entails risk of considerable disappointment, merits continuous investment and requires perseverance and patience.

WOLF IN THE SNOW

WARREN TALLMAN

PART ONE: FOUR WINDOWS ONTO LANDSCAPES

To enter the fictional house these novels form is to take up place in rooms where windows open out upon scenes in Saskatchewan, Quebec and Nova Scotia: two prairie towns, one farm, a small seacoast city and St. Urbain Street in Montreal. In order to prevent view from jostling view it is convenient to single out the characters Philip Bentley (*As For Me and My House*), Brian O'Connal (*Who Has Seen the Wind*), David Canaan (*The Mountain and the Valley*), Alan MacNeil (*Each Man's Son*) and Duddy Kravitz (*The Apprenticeship of Duddy Kravitz*), letting their lives suggest the details which make up the study. Since these five form into a handful, it is best to enter the fictional house at once and move across rooms to where the windows open out.

From whichever window one chooses to look, at whichever person, the initial impression gained is that of his isolation. Superficially, this isolation traces to the ways in which each is alienated from the natural childhood country of ordinary family life. In *As For Me and My House,* Philip Bentley has this comfort stolen from him even before it is provided when his unmarried father, a divinity student, turned atheist, turned artist, dies before Philip is born. That the son is cast by this deprivation into the limbo of an uncreated childhood becomes evident when he emerges into adult life also a divinity student, turned atheist, turned artist, struggling without success to dis-

"Wolf in the Snow," by Warren Tallman. In *Canadian Literature* 5 (Summer 1960), pp. 7-20 and 6 (Autumn 1960), pp. 41-48. By permission of Warren Tallman.

cover the father he did not know while married to a woman who is all too obviously more a mother to him than she is a wife.

In *The Mountain and the Valley,* David Canaan is gifted with yet cursed by reactions far too intense ever to mesh except occasionally with the more ordinary responses of his brother, sister, parents and grandmother. When he fails in a school play, his family has no resources with which to meet the violence of humiliation which fairly explodes within him. His childhood and youth are a long succession of such intensities leading to such explosions. Each time the pieces settle back together, he finds himself inched unwillingly away from others onto a precarious plane of solitary being from which he can communicate his extravagant reactions only by other extravagances which further emphasize his growing isolation.

If David's is the most painful face turned toward us, Brian O'Connal's is the most deceptive. Even as *Who Has Seen the Wind* opens, he is shown growing away from his family in order to follow impulses which bring his struggling consciousness into contact with what are described in the preface as "the realities of birth, hunger, satiety, eternity, death." But if Brian appears to discern a deeper than familial ordering of experience in and around the Saskatchewan town where he grows up, the persons and personifications which illustrate his discernment tell, I think, quite another story. They tell of a sensitive boy's attempts to reconcile himself to the human viciousness and natural desolation which characterize the town and the prairie. Of this conflict, more in place. Unlike Philip, David and Brian, Alan MacNeil in *Each Man's Son* is less an individualized child and more simply the naive witness to a stylized pattern of adult conflict. Thus he is the puppet son to each of three disparate fathers: Doctor Ainslee, the type of inhibited intellect; Archie MacNeil, the type of unthinking animal force; and the Gallic Louis Camire, the type of passionate spontaneity. Because the larger human pattern of which these men are parts has been broken, each partial man struggles toward a different solution to his incompletion, one which excludes the others. When their longings for wholeness draw them to Alan and his mother, the pattern will no longer knit. Alan's role as each man's son is to witness the gradual forcing together of these disastrously alienated men.

The kinds of alienation which I have sketched point to a common problem. When the hazards of life reach out to disrupt families and isolate children it is almost certain that such children will respond with attempts to create a self strong enough to endure the added stress and more extreme fluctuations of experience. Yet the very disturbances which create a need for such strength frequently conspire to take away the opportunity. Prematurely conscious of weakness in the face of experience, the timid self stands back from contention. And much of the isolation is in the standing back. Yet to lose out in this way is to gain in another. For so persistent and powerful are the mysterious forces which drive self on its journeys toward some measure of fulfillment that when the journey is interrupted self will either struggle to make the island upon which it finds itself habitable, or—if particularly hard-pressed —may strike out for new islands of its own making. To know experience or novels even cursorily is to realize that such attempts are among the decisive gestures of human experience. The more vital the attempt, the more interesting the discoveries, the more illuminating the journeys. But to say all this and then turn to Philip, David, Brian and Alan is to encounter difficulties.

First Brian. Throughout *Who Has Seen the Wind* we are shown his growing consciousness of the grim passive cruelty of the prairie and of the only somewhat less grim active cruelties of the community. The prairie doesn't care and the townspeople care too much, but in all of the wrong ways. Mitchell would have us understand that Brian attains insight into deep permanent forces of man and nature and so becomes reconciled to the problems of his existence. But if the winds and gods of the prairie and the town are shown ministering to the evolution of a troubled boy's consciousness, there are many reasons to question the nature of their influence. For what Brian actually discovers and enters into is somewhat uneasy communication with a hierarchy of odd and withdrawn persons, most of them caught up as he is in attempting to resolve the dilemma of their alienation from the community. At the head of this hierarchy are several disaffected persons whose professional standing gives them precarious half-footing in the community: Hislop, the enlightened minister who is forced to leave; Doctor Svarich; Miss Thompson, the school teacher with whom he has had an unsuccessful love affair elsewhere; and Digby, the school principal. Because these humane persons are only half accepted by a community which they in turn only half accept, they lead incomplete, almost inert lives.

Brian's more active education begins where their influence leaves off; with his uncle Sean, whose intelligent efforts to cope with the drouth are met by a human inertia so perverse that he is reduced to random cursing; with Milt Palmer, the shoe and harness maker, who eases his discontent with the jug he keeps under the counter in his shop and the copy of Berkeley's philosophy he reads and discusses with Digby, presumably to get at the nature of existence, actually to escape the pointlessness of the existence he leads; with Ben, the town ne'er-do-well, who makes his still and his gifts as a raconteur the basis for contact with a community that otherwise despises him; with the son, young Ben, who responds to his father's disgrace by a withdrawal so marked that his human impulses only glimmer at depths of his remote eyes; and with old Sammy, the town idiot, who lives almost totally withdrawn in a self-built insane asylum at the outskirts of town, his intelligence—that light which keeps the human psyche habitable—lost in the nightmare clutter which existence becomes when the light flickers out.

It is all but impossible to accept Mitchell's inference that contact with these persons serves to reconcile Brian's consciousness to the "realities of birth, hunger, satiety, eternity, death." What he learns, if anything, is that the kinds of suffering which afflict those who are completely alienated from the community are far more damaging than the kinds of suffering which afflict those who are only partly alienated. It isn't surprising that the two most vivid portraits in the novel are those of young Ben

and old Sammy, the two most severely withdrawn of all the persons represented. Young Ben appears to Brian in unexpected places and at unpredictable moments with all of the suddenness of a hallucination projected from Brian's unconscious. To be Brian in the kind of community Mitchell represents is to be not far from young Ben. And what is old Sammy in his age and insanity but young Ben later on and farther out on the road leading away from contact with other human beings. What but negative lessons can Brian learn from such dissociated beings —so grim a school of lives!

Nor is it possible to accept the protective, but not very protective, screen of humour with which Mitchell has softened and attempted to humanize the world Brian experiences. Here contrast is helpful. The mordant western humour of Mark Twain, Ambrose Bierce and Bret Harte derives the tensions which make it effective from these writers' awareness of the overt savagery of the settlement years. In Brian's world the savagery is still there—the gratuitous cruelty of the community drives the Chinese restaurant owner to despair and suicide— but it has become socially organized, hence acceptable. Mrs. Abercrombie, the town assassin, is also the town social leader. However, the intended humour of the scenes in which her control over the school board is finally broken is without animation because it is without true animosity. The firing of the enlightened minister, the exclusion of the Chinese children from the community, the suicide of their father, the sadistic persecution of Young Ben, as well as the constant badgering of the school teachers, provide cause enough for any amount of enmity. But far from being a gesture of delight at the downfall of a despicable person, the humour is simply a droll and softening pretense that she never was actually dangerous.

The need for this pretense is not far to seek or at least to suspect. If the town is presided over by Mrs. Abercrombie, an incarnation of community enmity toward personality—let them be citizens instead—the prairie is presided over by old Sammy, an incarnation of the disintegration which is likely to overtake all but the most resourceful personalities when the individual self wanders beyond the sphere of human community. These two represent the actual, the most powerful of the gods who preside over Brian's attempt to establish contact with human and natural forces which will sustain his precocious selfhood. And despite her overt hatred of the diversity and freedom that are essential for self-nurture, Mrs. Abercrombie is less fearsome than is old Sammy who presides with his mad, mumbled incantations over psychic chaos and old night. Or let us say that the open emptiness of the prairie is humanly more frightening than the huddled pettiness of the town. Because this is so, the town must be sugar coated with humour so that the lacklustre perversity of the place will seem merely droll, hence bearable. But readers who find it impossible to swallow Mrs. Abercrombie under any circumstances at all will feel that the failure of the humour reflects a failure of the novel to confront the actuality which it suggests. As a place for Brian to discover a community which will foster self-growth, the town in its resourcelessness more nearly resembles the prairie. The humour is scarcely a compensation for such desolation.

To turn to the more severe isolation from which David Canaan suffers in *The Mountain and The Valley* is to encounter a more intense but scarcely a more successful attempt to discover new ground upon which the withdrawn self might stand in its efforts to move into presence. During his childhood and youth David's vivid impulses fascinate his family and friends. Mutual responsiveness brings on that gradual blur of familiarity which can cause us to notice least those persons we know best; but when responsiveness is somehow short-circuited the one who stands apart becomes impressive in his otherness. Throughout childhood and early youth David moves among others with the aura about him of the chosen person, the mysterious Nazarite who is emotional toward an unknowable destiny by unseen gods. But what is an advantage during his early years becomes a disadvantage later when the appealing mystery of his loneliness becomes the oppressive ordeal of his unbreakable solitude. More devastating still, at no point in his life is he capable of actions which might rescue him from the limbo in which he dwells.

He carries on a correspondence and later a friendship with the Halifax boy, Toby, but makes no attempt to visit Toby and explore possibilities for new experience in the city. He is conscious of talents which might open experience out for him so that his self could follow into presence. But he turns his back upon these talents and remains on the farm even though aware that it is his prison rather than his promised land. He quarrels with his parents but seems unable to move past the evident incest barriers which bind him to them even as they shut him away from them. That the male mountain and the female valley of the title loom up so prominently in the novel is surely a sign, here as with Wordsworth, that natural objects have been endowed with all the seeming numinousness of their inaccessible human equivalents. Conversely, other persons in the novel are invested with a deceptive glamour. The breath of life fans the nucleus of David's impulses into a glow, but because these impulses are checked, they never achieve the release of communication, much less communion. Unable to know his family in their ordinariness, he must create his own knowledge in the image of his arrested, his childish and childlike psychic life. Consequently his parents are perceived as mythical, almost biblical beings and this appearance is sustained as long as David's response is intense enough, the glow white hot. Such intensities are as much the hallmark of the novel as a markedly devitalized humour is the hallmark of Mitchell's. But like Mitchell's humour, the intensity is badly flawed.

For David is trying to sustain an illusion. Whenever the hot impulse cools, the glow goes out of the novel and we see David's family and friends for what they are, very unbiblical, unmythical, ordinary human beings. At no time does his friend Toby demonstrate those distinguished qualities with which David invests him. His sister Anna is represented as soul of David's soul, but it is only possible for David to sustain this sublimated conception by overlooking the almost overtly incestuous basis for their relationship. Only the looming mountain can provide adequate expression for the childlike awe with which he regards his father. In his relations with others David is much like one inside a house which he cannot leave, looking out at persons he has never known because he has never actually moved among them. As one by one these persons depart, he begins to notice the emptiness, room leading silently to room. The novel is an account of David's attempt to ward off such knowledge. But fathers and mothers die, and brothers, friends and sisters—soul of his soul—depart. Until only the grandmother is left, calling out "Where is that child?" even as the child, unable to endure both an outer and an inner emptiness, goes at last up the snow-covered mountain into the final dimension of his solitude. The emptiness, the silence and the snow into which he sinks down at the end of the novel figure forth the constant nothingness against which his bright intensities had beat, thinking it the high shores of this actual world. His life would be pathetic if it were not heroic.

The heroism is in his effort, in the extreme tenacity with which David clings to the sources of his suffering, and it is in the novel, in the record of that suffering. The very intensity which creates those illusions with which David tries to live also creates a distinctive lyric exaltation. Because perception is so consistently at fever pitch, the descriptive surfaces of the novel are exceptionally fine-grained, the communion with nature, with appearances, with actions, so close that many passages read like lyric poems. But paradoxes are endless, and if the unreleased intensity which is a tragedy for David becomes an advantage for the novelist it in turn becomes another kind of disadvantage for the reader. For Buckler has no compositional key except maximum intensity. Sentence after sentence is forced to a descriptive pitch which makes the novel exceptionally wearing to read.

One turns with something like relief from the kind of illusions with which Brian O'Connal and David Canaan seek to escape isolation to the blunt but subtle absence of such illusions in *As For Me and My House*. The bleak assumption of this beauti-

ful novel is that Philip Bentley has no ground whatsoever upon
which he might stand, no communion at all through which he
might discover saving dimensions of self. The overwhelming
desolation which rims Horizon around—the hostile wind, the
suffocating dust and sand and the even more suffocating and
claustrophobic heat—recurs on the pages of Mrs. Bentley's
diary as outward manifestation of the inner desolation felt by
her husband. All that Philip can claim or cling to is his mad-
deningly inarticulate impulse to create. The novel is less like
a story than it is like a cumulative picture in which Ross, by
a remarkable, almost *tour de force* repetition of detail, grains
a central scene upon the reader's consciousness so that all
other details and even the action of the novel achieve meaningful focus in relation to the one scene at the centre, repeated
some thirty times. It is of course that in which Philip is shown
retreating to his study where he will sit, interminable evening
super-imposed upon interminable evening, drawing or fiddling
at drawing, or staring with baffled intensity at drawings he has
in some other time and place tried to draw. Yet, "Even though
the drawings are only torn up or put away to fill more boxes
when we move, even though no one ever gets a glimpse of
them—still they're for him the only part of life that's real or
genuine." The novel is a projection through the medium of
Mrs. Bentley's remarkably responsive consciousness of the despair in which her husband is caught, "some twisted, stumbling
power locked up within him—so blind and helpless it can't
find outlet, so clenched with urgency it can't release itself." And
the town itself, with the dust "reeling in the streets," the heat
"dry and deadly like a drill" and the wind "like something solid
pressed against the face," is simply a place named for the limbo
in which Bentley lives, "a wilderness outside of night and sky
and prairie with this one little spot of Horizon hung up lost
in its immensity" beneath which "he's as lost and alone."

Philip's need to escape from this isolation drives him to art.
But just as he can find no terms under which he may act as a
self so he can find no terms under which he may act as an
artist. His most characteristic drawing is a receding perspective

in which a looming false-front building gives way to a diminished next building, and a next, and a next, an endless progression which provides a portrait of the monotony of his own being. The novel is a study of a frustrated artist—actually, a non-artist—one unable to discover a subject which will release him from his oppressive incapacity to create. The excellence of the study traces to the remarkable resourcefulness with which Ross brings into place the day-to-day nuances of Mrs. Bentley's struggling consciousness as he builds up her account of an artist who cannot create because he cannot possess himself and who cannot possess himself because there is no self to possess. Certainly there are more deep-reaching portraits of the artist, for in this novel all is muffled within Philip's inarticulation, but none that I know represents with so steady a pressure of felt truth the pervasive undermining of all vital energies which occurs when the would-be artist's creativity is thwarted. No momentary exuberance survives. The flowers won't grow. The adopted boy, for whom Philip tries to provide that childhood he did not have himself, cannot be kept. Neither can his horse. Neither can his dog. Nothing can drive away the "faint old smell of other lives" from the house. No one and nothing can intercede to shut out the wind, prevent the dust, lessen the heat in which the Bentleys are "imbedded . . . like insects in a fluid that has congealed." Not once in the novel does Philip break through the torment of his constraint to utter a free sentence. Even when his wife confronts him with knowledge of his covert love affair with Judith West his response, beyond the endurance of even an Arthur Dimmesdale, is silence. But if the beauty is in the detailing, it does not trace to the dreariness which is portrayed. It traces to the constant presence in Mrs. Bentley's consciousness of an exuberance which flares up like matches in the wind and struggles to survive, a counter-impulse within her by which life attempts to defeat the defeat. This bravery loses out to the dreariness—the flowers *won't* grow—but in the process of struggling it animates the novel.

However, there is no mistaking the meaning which events

bring into place during the last distraught days which the diary records when Judith West dies and even the wind rebels, blowing the false-front town flat. When creative power is thwarted, destructive power emerges. "It's hard," Mrs. Bentley tells us, "to stand back watching a whole life go to waste." But the diary is an inch-by-inch representation along the walls of her resisting consciousness of the relentless crumbling under destructive pressure of her husband's life and hence her own, as the undertow of bitter silence about which the portrait is built drags these prairie swimmers under wind, under dust, under heat, to that ocean floor of inner death upon which such silence rests, strongest swimmers most deeply drowned.

There is a superb scene in which the Bentleys walk during an April snow storm to the outskirts of town:

The snow spun around us thick and slow like feathers till it seemed we were walking on and through a cloud. The little town loomed up and fell away. On the outskirts we took the railroad track, where the telegraph poles and double line of fence looked like a drawing from which all the horizontal strokes had been erased. The spongy flakes kept melting and trickling down our cheeks, and we took off our gloves sometimes to feel their coolness on our hands. We were silent most of the way. There was a hush in the snow like a finger raised.

We came at last to a sudden deep ravine. There was a hoarse little torrent at the bottom, with a shaggy, tumbling swiftness that we listened to a while, then we went down the slippery bank to watch. We brushed off a stone and sat with our backs against the trestle of the railway bridge. The flakes came whirling out of the whiteness, spun against the stream a moment, vanished at its touch. On our shoulders and knees and hats again they piled up little drifts of silence.

Then the bridge over us picked up the coming of a train. It was there even while the silence was still intact. At last we heard a distant whistle-blade, then a single point of sound, like one drop of water in a whole sky. It dilated, spread. The sky and silence began imperceptibly to fill with it. We steeled ourselves a little, feeling the pounding onrush in the trestle of the bridge. It quickened, gathered, shook the earth, then swept in an iron roar above us, thundering and dark.

We emerged from it slowly, while the trestle a moment or two sustained the clang and din. I glanced at Philip, then quickly back to the water. A train still makes him wince sometimes. At night, when the whistle's loneliest, he'll toss a moment, then lie still and tense. In the daytime I've seen his eyes take on a quick half-eager look, just for a second or two, and then sink flat and cold again.

The hushed, almost sealed, inner silence which is the price Philip Bentley pays for his failure to summon self into presence is not broken but poured momentarily full of the "iron roar . . . thundering and dark" which in times past had signalled to him an escape from the desolation of his childhood. Even on this forsaken April day it echoes into lost realms of self to those times when his eyes took on a "quick half-eager look" until the weight of silence reasserts itself and they turn "flat and cold" like the day. When an artist in fact discovers that close correspondence to life which he is always seeking, life takes over and the details of representation become inexhaustibly suggestive. D. H. Lawrence's unhappy lovers have wandered through Sherwood Forest to just such sudden "deep ravines" and have half glimpsed the "shaggy tumbling swiftness" which they, like the Bentleys, have lost from their lives. And James Joyce's depressed Dubliners have had the same universal angel of silence shake snow into drifts upon "shoulders and knees and hats" as the pounding onrush of the train, thunder in the blood, dwindles and disappears, leaving the scene, "distorted, intensified, alive with thin, cold bitter life." It is not surprising that the departing train draws Mrs. Bentley's thoughts—it is one pathos of the novel that we never learn her first name—back in the longest retrospective passage of the diary to her husband's childhood in search of the bitterness, constantly emphasized, which gradually seals him in, seals her out. Nor is it surprising that later when she becomes aware of the force of mute passion with which Judith West breaks through Philip's constraint she is at once reminded of the April day she and her husband "sat in the snowstorm watching the water rush through the stones" —the silence, the snow, the water and the stones—the story of their lives in a profound moment, a magnificent scene.

If knowledge of Philip Bentley's uncreated childhood comes mostly through the indirection of his adult life, our knowledge of Alan MacNeil's isolation and insecurity comes through the indirection of the adult conflicts he witnesses. And most of the adults in *Each Man's Son* can be known only through the additional indirection of the assigned part each plays in the general scheme of conflict which MacLennan has devised. They are like those persons in actual life whose roles become masks concealing self from access. Such arrangements are as unsatisfactory in novels as they are in actuality. Self is the centre of being, the source of our most vital impulses, and when those fictional persons who enact the artist's vision of life are not directly related to the artist's self, they will inevitably speak and act mechanically, without true animation. This is so decidedly the case in *Each Man's Son*—as in MacLennan's fiction as a whole—that any attempt to understand Alan MacNeil's plight must be an attempt to move past the masks MacLennan has created in order to reach what is vital, the source rather than the surfaces of his vision.

The mask in *Each Man's Son*—as, again, in all of MacLennan's novels—is made up of the pseudo-sophistication, the surface civilization in terms of which the portrait of Doctor Ainslee is built. MacLennan never wearies of extolling his surgical prowess and yet his human *savoir faire* and yet his intellectual probity. He is the fastest man in North America with an appendectomy and other doctors stand by, not to help, but to hold the watch on his performance, noting afterwards with knowing glances that Ainslee has done it again. If I seem to be suggesting that Doctor Ainslee is Walter Mitty played straight, this is less an accusation than it is an identification. For it is not, as MacLennan would have us believe, residual effects of Calvinistic sin which constantly unsettle the doctor's composure. It is the all but impossible façade he seeks to maintain, so false that MacLennan is incapable of animating it because it has so little to do with the profound naiveté and relative crudity of response in which MacLennan's true force as an artist is rooted.

If all the world were true there would be no place in fiction for falsity. But, notoriously, the world is far from true, and Doctor Ainslee's cultural veneer is all too accurate in its patent falsity—true of Ainslee, true of a good half of MacLennan's protagonists, true—above all—of most North Americans, who also adopt European disguises having little or nothing to do with the self beneath, the source of vital energy. Constant anxiety is the price Ainslee pays in order to maintain his façade. But if MacLennan would have us believe that the reason for the anxiety is the Calvinism, a more apt explanation for both the anxiety and the mask comes to us from the other, the vital side of the novel.

The night that Ainslee operates upon Alan he flees to the harbourside from the strain of both a professional and a personal involvement—cutting the child he hopes to adopt—and experiences a partial breakdown in which "his mind was pounding with its own rhythms and his body was out of control." To escape the panic that grips him, he runs up the wharf.

Before he realized that his feet had caught in something soft he plunged forward, an explosion of light burst in his head and his right temple hit the boards. For a moment he lay half stunned, trying to understand what had happened. He rolled to get up, and as he did so, the hair on the nape of his neck prickled. He had stumbled over something alive, and now this living thing was rising beside him. He could smell, feel and hear it, and as he jerked his head around he saw the outline of a broken-peaked cap appear against the residual light from the sea. It rose on a pair of huge shoulders and stood over Ainslee like a tower.

The tower is Red Willie MacIsaac, and Ainslee in his fear, repugnance and anger shouts out, "You drunken swine, MacIsaac—don't you know who I am?" This outcry under these circumstances does much to illuminate the novel.

For the drunken swine, Red Willie, is one of the group of incredibly naive and endlessly quarrelsome displaced Highlanders whose portraits in their really superb clarity and exuberance make up much the most vital part of the novel. These

Highlanders, doomed to wear their vitality away in the dreary Cape Breton Island mines, rebel like the profound children they are by recourse to the only political action of which they are capable, their endless evening brawls. The sum of their whimsical and powerful impulses is crystallized into the portrait of their downfallen hero, Archie MacNeil, the finest single portrait in MacLennan's novels.

Now the main use to which Doctor Ainslee's mask—his civilized façade—is put is to hold these impulses in check. A word from him and the miners back away, chagrined. When he cries out, Red Willie becomes contrite. But the identification is surely much closer. When the rhythms of Ainslee's mind and body become separated and he trips over and becomes mingled with Red Willie there is reason to believe that "this living thing . . . beside him" is simply the self behind the mask, the vital, violent being held in check by the civilized surface. That Ainslee can and does check Red Willie is an obvious victory for Ainslee and it is a tragedy for Alan's actual father, Archie. For Ainslee stumbles over Red Willie immediately after Archie has been ruinously defeated in Trenton. And the voice that emerges when he lies tangled with Red Willie mutters, "There was dirty tricks in the States last Friday and by chesus I am going to kick them up your ass." The blame is, if dubiously aimed, properly assigned. The conflict at the heart of the novel is between the civilized façade maintained by Ainslee and the naive violence of the place represented by Archie MacNeil.

Alan is caught between the violent needs which drive his father away on the forlorn prize fighter's Odyssey in which his one-time physical magnificence becomes the dupe of unscrupulous promoters and the counter needs which drive Ainslee to fill in the chinks of his cultural façade by inching his way through the alien Greek of the classical Odyssey. Both men want to save Alan from the mines, those holes in the ground which give nothing and take everything away, but each tries to do so in ways which rule out the other. At the conclusion of the novel, when Archie prevails and smashes down his wife

and her lover, and he and Ainslee confront each other, it is the
civilized surface confronting the violent self among the ruins
created by their tragic alienation.

To read novels is to gain impressions and these are what I
tried to document in the first part of this essay. Now let the
four windows of the fictional house become as one view and
let the four occupants (Alan MacNeil from *Each Man's Son,*
Philip Bentley from *As For Me and My House,* David Canaan
from *The Mountain and the Valley* and Brian O'Connal from
Who Has Seen the Wind) be regrouped in a scene where the
intangible which I have been calling "self" looks toward other
intangibles which most decisively influence its efforts to come
into "presence." At the back depth of this scene an immeasur-
able extent of snow is falling in a downward motion that is
without force through a silence that is without contrasts to an
earth that is "distorted, intensified, alive with thin, cold, bitter
life." How bitter can best be shown by lifting the snow shroud
to let the sun shine momentarily as Morley Callaghan's three
hunters (*They Shall Inherit the Earth*) move across "rocky
ridges and the desolate bush" to where a herd of deer whose
hooves had become caught in the snow crust now lie in bloody
heaps, abandoned where they have been destroyed by a pack
of thin, cold, bitter wolves. As the hunters watch, the sun sets,
and "a vast shadow fell over the earth, over the rocky ridges
and the desolate bush and over the frozen carcasses." The
night shadows mingle with the wolf shadows and cover over the
dark blood of the deer as the wavering shroud of snow again begins to fall through the "dreadful silence and coldness" felt
everwhere at the back depth of the scene.

Move now to the middle depth, where from the left a bleak
expanse of prairie gives way at the centre to forests and mountains which merge on the right with the seacoast looking toward
Europe where Alan stands with his mother as he did the day

his novel began. That day, Alan emulated Yeats' sad shepherd from the opposite Irish shore, but in Alan's shell the "inarticulate moan" which the shepherd heard becomes that "oldest sound in the world," the remote waterfall roaring of his own salt blood. When Yeats' shepherd grew and changed into an ominous older man the sound in the shell darkened and strengthened into the beating of a prophetic "frenzied drum" which later still became a "blood-dimmed tide" carrying to the Europe of his imagination as to the Europe of succeeding years "the fury and the mire of human veins." But in Alan's less tutored ear, on his side of the Atlantic, the blood sea sounds a more innocent summons as his thoughts follow along those unseen paths wandered by his bright and battered highland father. All Alan knows is that this father is the "strongest man in the world." All that this strongest man knows is the inner thrust of a ceaseless, mindless desire to prevail so powerful that even as he stumbles from defeat to defeat he follows this path down as though it were a way up to the championship, that mountain peak in the mind from which no opposing force could ever banish him. And so powerful is the son's consciousness of his father's destiny that even at the last when "the pack of muscles under the cloth of his jacket shifted" and the "poker shot up," Alan's immediate thought, far off from the murder at hand, is, "So that was what it meant to be the strongest man in the world!"

The desire to prevail. Move to where David Canaan is standing in a field beside the tracks as the train taking his friend Toby back to Halifax "came in sight thundering nearer and nearer." But Toby, whom David had expected to wave as the train drew past, "didn't glance once, not once, toward the house or the field." And as the thunder on the tracks diminishes, the thunder in David's blood takes over and "a blind hatred of Toby went through him. It seemed as if that were part of his own life he was seeing — his life stolen before his eyes." His protest at being cancelled out rises from hatred to rage and he "slashed at the pulpy turnips blindly wherever the hack fell," until he slashes his way through the rage and discovers a deeper

depth where "in his mind there was only a stillness like the stillness of snow sifting through the spokes of wagon wheels or
moonlight on the frozen road or the dark brook at night."

At the far left, the prairies slope away like Shelley's "lone
and level sands." But there is no fallen Ozymandias here where
no Ozymandias has ever stood. Instead there are the false-
front stores of Horizon, warped by the heat, sand-blasted by the
drouth dust, and blown askew by the prairie wind. Here, Mrs.
Bentley walks once more—as in her diary she so often mentions—along the tracks to the outskirts of town where five
grain elevators stand "aloof and imperturbable, like ancient
obelisques," as dust clouds "darkening and thining and swaying" in the ominous upper prairie of the sky seem "like a quiver-
ing backdrop before which was about to be enacted some grim,
primeval tragedy." The swaying dust clouds above, the darkening prairie beneath, the ancient-seeming elevators she huddles
against, as well as her mournful sense of the grim, the primeval,
the tragic—these details speak for the entire scene which I
have been sketching. They speak of a tragedy in which the
desire to prevail that drives self on its strange journeys toward
fulfillment is brought to an impasse on northern fields of a continent which has remained profoundly indifferent to its in-
habitant, transplanted European man. The continent itself—
the gray wolf whose shadow is underneath the snow—has
resisted the culture, the cultivation, the civilization which is
indigenous to Europe but alien to North America even though
it is dominant in North America.

If Alan, Philip, Brian and David are notably unable to discover alternatives to the isolation from which they suffer, this
is not because they are resourceless persons but because the
isolation is ingrained, inherent, indwelling. One alternative is
much like the next when all the rooms are equally empty in the
vast space-haunted house they occupy. And those gods who
overrule the house toward whom self quickens in its need to
prevail are such as preside over forests and open fields, mountains, prairies and plains: snow gods, dust gods, drought gods,
wind gods, wolf gods—native to the place and to the empty

manner born. These divinities speak, if at all, to all such as lone it toward the mountain pass and the hidden lake, the rushing river and the open empty road. And the experiential emptiness of the place shows on the faces of such loners as that weathered yet naive expressionlessness, the stamp of the man to whom little or nothing has happened in a place where the story reads, not here, not much, not yet. Underneath the European disguises North American man assumes, self too is such a loner. And the angel at his shoulder, met everywhere in the weave of these novels because it is everywhere and omnipresent in the vast house we occupy, is silence. Out of the weave of the silence emerges the shroud of snow. But underneath the snow, the dark blood brightens.

For self does not readily accept separation, isolation and silence. These are conditions of non-being, and whether one assumes that the ground toward which self struggles in its search for completion is divine and eternal or only individual and temporal, either alternative supposes rebellion against no being at all. It's from this fate that Brian O'Connal flees in panic the night he walks from his uncle's farm to town. "It was as though he listened to the drearing wind and in the spread darkness of the prairie night was being drained of his very self." It is against this same fate that Alan MacNeil's father beats with his fists, seeking some eminence from which the physical strength that is his measure of self cannot be pulled down to defeat. It is against this fate that Philip Bentley struggles those evenings in his study, seeking to liberate "some twisted stumbling" creative power locked up within him even though all he can create is sketches which reveal how pervasively non-being has invaded his life. And it is against this fate that David Canaan slashes in the field beside the tracks before yielding when he lies down against the flank of the mountain under a blanket of snow upon a bed of silence.

But it is not here that the scene dims out. For the last sound that David hears is that North American lullaby which sings the sleeping self awake as a train "whistled beyond the valley" then "thundered along the rails and was gone." Had

Alan MacNeil turned his back upon Europe, the blood sound in the shell would have been that rising up from the railroad earth, those train sounds hooting all loners home to where, up front in the scene, the dark silence breaks up into the gushing of the neon and the noise.

But along St. Urbain street in Montreal, the marvellous, the splendid and the amazing have given way to the commonplace, the shabby and the unspeakable. And even before thinking of anything so portentous as a new self, Mordecai Richler has been engaged in the much more onerous task of clearing away the debris which has accumulated in a world where all disguises have been put in doubt. His first three novels are studies of ruined lives: André, the guilt-haunted Canadian artist, who is eventually murdered by the Nazi, Kraus, whose sister Theresa then commits suicide; the guilt-ridden homosexual, Derek, his equally guilty sister, Jessie, and her equally guilty husband, the acoholic, Barney; the Wellington College professor, Theo Hall, and his wife, Miriam; Norman, the American Fifth Amendment expatriate whose brother is murdered by Ernst, the German youth whom Sally, the Toronto girl, ruins her life trying to save. All of these persons reach out, cry out, for any masks other than the ones they have.

And they testify to Richler's affinity with that side of modern life where the misbegotten wander through ruined Spains of self-pity, poisoned to the point of near, and at times actual, madness by self-loathing. However, Richler does not seek out these persons in order to demonstrate several times over that we are wrapped up like so many sweating sardines in world misery, world guilt, world sorrow. Like André, Norman and Noah, the protagonists of these novels, he is inside the misery looking for a way out. What looks out is a courageous intelligence struggling to realize that the tormented sleep of self-loathing which he explores is just that—a sleep, a dream, a nightmare: but not the reality.

In his fourth novel, *The Apprenticeship of Duddy Kravitz*, the sleeper begins to come awake. The nightmare is still there, but it is not the same nightmare. In *The Acrobats* and *A Choice of Enemies,* Richler chooses areas of world guilt as the basis for dream terror. The Spanish war, the second world war, the victims of these wars and of their ideologies make up the manifest content, the general human failure which images and invites the latent personal failures represented. People whose lives have gone smash drift into areas where life has gone smash and consort with the ghosts who have survived. In *Duddy Kravitz* the scope contracts. Both the ghosts who make up the nightmare and the ideologies through which they wander have faded from mind. Duddy's father, his brother Lenny, his uncle and aunt, his teacher MacPherson, his friend Virgil, his enemy Dingleman, and his shiksa Yvette all live tangled lives in a world where they do not know themselves. But they are caught up by personal disorders rather than world disorders, family strife rather than international strife, individual conflict rather than ideological conflict. And within the localized dream we meet an entirely different dreamer. We meet the direct intelligence and colloquial exuberance that is Duddy's style—and Richler's.

T. S. Eliot has said that poetry in our time is a mug's game. So is fiction, and Richler is one of the mugs. Duddy has ceased to care for appearances and this insouciance releases him from nightmare. All of the other people in the novel cannot possess themselves because their vital energies are devoted full-time to maintaining the false appearances in terms of which they identify themselves. These appearances—the cultural, ethical, communal pretensions to which they cling—mask over but scarcely conceal the distinctly uncultured, unethical, isolated actuality in which they participate. Hence the importance in their lives of Dingleman, the Boy Wonder, who is a projection of their actual longings to be at ease in Zion in a Cadillac at the same time as he is a projection of the limitation of these longings, being hopelessly crippled. But Duddy, who has ceased to care for appearances, sees people for what they are, himself included. And what he sees, he accepts—himself included. In an acquisitive world he is exuberantly acquisitive. When he is tricked, he weeps. When threatened, he becomes dangerous. When attacked, he bites back. When befriended, he is generous. When hard-pressed he becomes frantic. When denied, he is filled with wrath. From the weave of this erratic shuttling, a self struggles into presence, a naive yet shrewd latter-day Huck Finn, floating on a battered money raft down a sleazy neon river through a drift of lives, wanting to light out for somewhere, wanting somewhere to light out for.

Plato tells us that when a new music is heard the walls of the city tremble. The music in Duddy Kravitz is where in novels it always is, in the style. The groove in which the style runs is that of an exuberance, shifting into exaggeration, shifting into those distortions by which Richler achieves his comic vision of Montreal. The finest parts of the novel are those in which Richler most freely indulges the distortions: the sequence in which the documentary film director Friar produces a wedding ceremony masterpiece which views like the stream of consciousness of a lunatic, a fantasia of the contemporary mind; the entire portrait of Virgil who wants to organize the epileptics of the world and be "their Sister Kenny," as well as the more sombre portraits of Dingleman and Duddy's aunt Ida. Because Duddy has ceased to care for appearances, he moves past all of the genteel surfaces of the city and encounters an actuality in which all that is characteristically human has retreated to small corners of consciouness, and life becomes a grotesque game played by bewildered grotesques. The persons who make up this gallery not only fail to invoke self but can scarcely recognize what it is to be a human being. They are like uncertain creatures in a fabulous but confusing zoo, not sure why they are there, not even sure what human forest they once inhabited.

They testify in the language of the sometimes comic, sometimes grim, distortions Richler has created to the oppressive weight of doubt, guilt, remorse, shame and regret that history has imposed upon modern man, particularly upon man in the city, where the effects of history, most closely organized, are most acutely felt. The greater the system of threats to self, the more extensive the system of appearances needed to ward off those threats, the more marked the distortions of character-istic human need and desire. And the more marked the distor-tions, the more difficult the artist's task. For sensibility, that active sum of the artist's self, never does exist in relation to itself alone. It exists in relation to what is—actual persons, an actual city, actual lives. When the impact of accomplished history imposes distortions upon that actuality, sensibility must adjust itself to the distortions. The story of these adjustments is, I think, the most significant feature of North American fiction in our time. Long ago and far away, before World War One o'clock, Theodore Dreiser could look at the world with direct eyes. Characteristic human impulses of love, sorrow, hope, fear, existed in the actual world as love, sorrow, hope, fear; and Dreiser could direct his powerful sensibility into represen-tation which was, as they say, "like life." But after World War One, in *The Great Gatsby,* possibly the most significant of the between-wars novels, there is open recognition of a distorted actuality necessitating a reordering of sensibility, one which both Gatsby and Fitzgerald fail to achieve.

Since World War Two the need for adjustment has become even more marked, simply because the distortions have become more pronounced. In *Duddy Kravitz,* Richler follows closely in the groove of Duddy's exuberance and on out into the exag-gerations and distortions which make up his adjustment to actual Montreal. By doing so he is able to achieve an authentic relationship to life in that city—Duddy's dream of Caliban along the drear streets of Zoo. In this Richler is at one with the considerable group of contemporary writers—call them mugs, call them angry, call them beat—who all are seeking in their art those readjustments which will permit them to relate their sensibilities to what actually is. History has had and con-tinues to have her say. These writers are trying to answer back. If the vision which Richler achieves in answer to history jars upon our sensibilties, that is because we have all heard of Prospero's cloud-capped towers and gorgeous palaces. Yet, if the style which conveys the vision twangles from glib to brash, from colloquial to obscene, that is because the true North

American tone, at long past World War Two o'clock, is much closer to that of Caliban than ever it has been to that of Prospero whose magic was a European magic, long sunk from sight, and whose daughter and her beau and their world are out of fashion like old tunes or like the lovers on Keats' urn, maybe forever but address unknown. The brave new world toward which Duddy's self quickens is the lake property he covets throughout the novel and finally possesses. When he dives in, seeking a rebirth, he scrapes the bottom. But he doesn't care, he doesn't care, he doesn't care. Which is why the mug can make with the music.

D. H. Lawrence contended that in the visions of art a relatively finer vision is substituted for the relatively cruder visions extant. But in North America, as I hope this restricted study at least partially confirms, finer is relatively crude, because frequently untrue, and crude can be relatively fine. All to often, in fiction as in life, those pretensions which we seek out because they make us fine provide false furnishings for the actual house in which we live. This fine is crude. Duddy, who would not know a pretension if he met one, wanders for this reason by accident and mostly unaware into the actual house. His crude is relatively fine. True, there are no gods hovering over Duddy's lake, no grandiose hotel, no summer camp for children. There is only old mother North America with her snow hair, her mountain forehead, her prairie eyes, and her wolf teeth, her wind songs and her vague head of old Indian memories. And what has she to do with Duddy Kravitz? A lot, I think. For when the house is repossessed the gods come back—snow gods, dust gods, wind gods, wolf gods—but life gods too. And life is the value. When history conspires against life, ruining the house, life will fight back in the only way it can, by not caring. Heavy, heavy doesn't hang over Duddy's head. And that is his value.

Snow melts away. Mountains can be very beautiful. Wheat is growing on the prairies. And in the dark forest beside the hidden lakes the deer are standing, waiting. So turn off the neon, tune out the noise, and place Duddy in the foreground of the scene. Since life is the value, let blood melt snow, and place David Canaan beside him. Strike a match to light Mrs. Bentley a path through the wolf-wind night with its dust-grit teeth until she appears standing beside Duddy and David. Smooth over that bashed-in face, those cauliflowered ears, and let Highland Archie MacNeil, strongest man in the world, appear. For this reader it is these four who emerge from the novels considered as crude with the true crudeness of the place, and by this token most fine, most worth close consideration by those who take the visions of fiction as a decisive mode of relatedness to the actual house in which we live. And of these four, it is Mrs. Bentley in her utter absence of pretentiousness and Duddy in his utter absence of pretentiousness who most effectively and convincingly come forward and take their awkward North American bows. At which point, close out the scene.

MY SECOND BOOK

ERNEST BUCKLER

January 30, 1967

Dear Greg:

This is really just a postscript to the letter I sent you the other day—which I had written and mailed just before your second letter came.

Re. The Cruelest Month; I thought I had a file of comment on it somewhat like I had on the others, but if I had I simply can't locate it. Butter firkins do *not* provide the best filing system. But a few things do occur to me. I first called it The Cells of Love; the idea being that "cells" could be interpreted in either meaning; as the constituent parts or as a place of incarceration almost. Beyond this, it was supposed (if I remember rightly) to take up a lot of other things along the way. What happens when people face their own bones, really, and how they come out of the confrontation. (Morse faces the death of talent, Paul physical death—and also the maybe death of his always sustaining belief in the need to stand upright-alone without support, Rex the death of charm and of love (Sheila's) etc.) The question of change; do people, ever, much? The tempering of the fire, and its somewhat ironic results. (When you see someone maybe made over the way you'd thought you wanted them to be, do they seem suddenly worse? Kate's reaction to Morse's almost "soft" idealism at the end, her notice of her almost silliness with love; the irony that Paul thinks he's found an answer in Letty—when, anyone should see, particularly with Letty changing herself ("proper" speech, etc.), that

From a copy of a letter to Gregory M. Cook from Ernest Buckler. In *Ernest Buckler: His Creed and Craft,* an unpublished Master's thesis, Department of English, Acadia University (May 1967), pp. 286-87. By permission of Ernest Buckler.

this is maybe an ignis fatuus too). The way people continue to fool themselves. A kind of thesis on writing itself, sex itself, reality itself. The idea that the only way to face this nihilistic world is with the grin or the fart (flatus, if one must euphemize); and yet that something in people that still instinctively honors courage. The desperate tyranny of the weak over the strong (Rex over Sheila). The seldom-realized tragedy of the old (Fennison, Sr.). The "reign of accident." Too much, really, all of this, in the one mouthful of a book—but, as who in the interview book said that in every novel one is perennially tempted to cover everything so that it will no longer be necessary to write another?[1]

All garbled, this, but if I come across anything more coherent later, I'll send it along.

Yours,

ERN

P.S. Also the idea of the soundness of the "natural" country person weighing more than the specious complexity & chatter (like people who can fart at will) of the sophisticated. (Though I'm not all so sure about this now. Not at all.)

---

[1] Francois Mauriac in *Writers at Work*. Edited by Malcolm Cowley (New York: Viking Press 1959), p. 44.

FIVE REVIEWS OF *THE CRUELEST MONTH*

1. VARIOUS KINDS OF LOVE

CLAUDE BISSELL

In ten years of reviewing Canadian fiction, the most important single event for me was the appearance in 1952 of Ernest Buckler's *The Mountain and the Valley*. This was, above all, a novel in depth; not, as most Canadian novels tended to be, a skimming of the surface of life, or a journalistic report of events and people, or a sentimental pastiche; but rather a reflective, poetic exploration of the human mind and soul under duress. After such a long period, the appearance of a second novel is a major event. I am happy to report that it is an event in the widest possible significance of the word, for *The Cruelest Month* is, like the first novel, an important book and an addition to our literature.

One must begin by saying that *The Cruelest Month* will not have the immediate appeal that *The Mountain and the Valley* had. In a sense, Buckler's first book was the novel that every man is said to contain within himself. Although it was not autobiographical, it did not stray far from the experience that the writer had felt and proved on his pulses. Sophisticated in technique and delicate and subtle in style, it was about simple and uncomplicated human beings in a simple and uncomplicated society. It was a novel about a period not far removed from the present in years, and yet in tone and texture of another era. The era is thus beautifully described by one of the characters in *The Cruelest Month*:

From "Canadian Books," a review by Claude Bissell. In *The Dalhousie Review* 43 (Winter 1963-64), pp. 566-69. By permission of Claude Bissell.

82

That was a different time in every way. The whole settlement lived in a kind of eternal and unaging present then. The trees and the fields no less than the people. There were no specialized and worldly knowledges to put one man ahead of the other. There was no ghost from the outmoding future then, to cast its shadow on the present and corrode it like a machine. There was no consciousness in anyone or anything, not even in the rocks, of Time's outmoding its very self. All things lived on the plain of a replete and self-renewing now, which stayed as young to the adult as it did to the child.

This passage contains the reflections of the one character in the new novel whose links are most clearly with the society of *The Mountain and the Valley*. The other characters, with the exception of one study in robust and healthy primitivism, come from outside the early society, and are, by comparison, intensely sophisticated. Three of them are Americans: a sardonic and embittered writer of worldly novels; a girl reared in the opulent gentility of the American East, but mercifully uncontaminated by her upbringing; her husband, of obscure lineage, with a physical grace unmarked by the slow stain of thought. There are three Canadians: a young man whose roots go deep into rural Nova Scotia society; an attractive spinster, the only daughter of a Dalhousie professor; and the central unifying character in the novel, a man who has breasted many experiences throughout the world, always emerging with a philosophic and humorous sense of acceptance.

A catalogue of the characters in the novel indicates the kind of complex problem that Buckler has set for himself, for most of the characters call for preliminary explanation and background material. They do not spring naturally into life, as did the characters in *The Mountain and the Valley*. But Buckler reduces the necessity for elaborate explanatory detail by bringing his characters together in an isolated Nova Scotian farmhouse situated, one suspects, not very far from the mountain and the valley of the first novel. The owner of the farmhouse is the philosophic adventurer who accepts only those guests who seek out his latter-day Walden. The main action of the book takes place during a period in April when awakening nature underlines awakening emotions. Each of the characters comes with a heavy burden: Paul, the owner, with a consciousness of the imminence of death; Kate, the spinster, with the memory of a beloved father's agonizing death-bed; Sheila, the socialite, and her wastrel husband, with a sense of the dwindling of their love; Morse, the novelist, with the conviction of failure and intellectual impotence; Bruce, the young farmer aspiring to be a doctor, with a corroding sense of guilt in the accident that has taken the life of his wife and child. In the permutations and combinations of emotion there are no startlingly overt events: Sheila and Bruce fall in love with each other and experience a brief, ecstatic passion; Paul returns from a check-up in Montreal more than ever conscious of the shadow of death; Rex, with a clumsy infantile bravado, attempts suicide, fails dismally, and recovers the love of his estranged wife. In the final scene there is a literal ordeal by fire, which resolves doubts and despairs and brings the action to a calm and cleansing conclusion.

In one sense this is a study in the various kinds of love between men and women. Although there are passages descriptive of physical love, some of them rising to heights of erotic lyricism, this is not a novel about the sweet mysteries of the flesh. Buckler is not writing about love as a release, or a triumph, but about love as a stubborn fact of human existence, no less restricting and confining than any other experience, love as "the charactered face of stoicism." In *The Mountain and the Valley* Buckler was concerned with the binding effect of the family despite the external sense of divisiveness and tension. In a sense he has returned to this theme in his new novel, but in a more complex and involved fashion; for the family of *The Mountain and the Valley* was a biological unit, bound together by ties of consanguinity and habit; the family of *The Cruelest Month* is one where the ties are those of suffering and understanding.

The theme, then, is an unusual and rich one, but it is not one calculated to arouse an instantaneous response from the reader, or to carry him along triumphantly in its wake. Moreover, the prose, which in the first novel could be at times tortuous and difficult has become far more complex, intense, and involved. The pursuit of the microscopic detail has become an obsession, and often brings the flow of the narrative to a halt. It is, none the less, the kind of obsession that great writers have. Buckler expresses his own apologia in these words that he gives to Morse, the novelist:

Granted that with the microscope your tool you engraved no more than a single comma of infinity on the head of a pin, how much better did the telescope serve you? What good was a bloody relief map if half the truth was in a blade of grass? When every damn thing in the world was *sui generis?* What good was an *outline* of the heart if the infinite sub-divisions of human feeling defied the microscope even?

One has the feeling that this is a novel written with the heart's blood, in constant fear that the vision may suddenly flee. The words of Buckler's fictional character become, one feels, the author's own *cri de coeur*:

Did she want to know what that was like—what it was like when a writer wasn't writing? The solid in you separated from the liquid, to form that paralytic guy sitting on your guts. And then you found they'd cut the cords on the little hammock that held your brain up and your brain had slipped down below your eyes. They'd cut your heel cords too and the hammock strings under your heart and they'd taken the balls out of your voice. The only thing they hadn't cut was the one nerve that smoulders when you watch yourself sitting helpless on your own guts—You were like one of those *days* that have no talent —that you try to drink away or sleep away but keep awaking to, dead sober. You couldn't force yourself to write. You could prop the words up on the page, yes; but they woudn't join hands. You knew the minute you put the paper away each letter in every word dropped down as dead as the spaces between them. That's what it was like when a writer wasn't writing.

The Cruelest Month represents an inevitable stage in the development of an artist. The first novel had the fluidity and lyric grace of autobiography. The structure was determined by the simple flow of events, and a strong emotional appeal was gained by a deep immersion in the consciousness of a central figure. The new novel is carefully, elaborately and a bit stiffly constructed. The centre of interest shifts rapidly from one character to another, and there is no strong centre. Something of the spirit of the novel is perhaps unconsciously revealed by the frequent use of mathematical metaphors to record the movement of emotions. All this, however, is the price that the artist pays for his attempt to escape from the terrible fluidity of confession. One feels that the poetry and the vision so beautifully captured in the first novel have not been completely captured in the second. But they are always hard by, waiting to surrender utterly to the subtlest sensibility of contemporary Canadian prose fiction.

---

2.   SOUND AND FURY

ROBERT HARLOW

In 1952 Ernest Buckler published *The Mountain and the Valley,* a novel which attracted a good deal of attention here and abroad. It established Buckler as an author of some potentiality and reputation. Now, eleven years later, he has brought forth *The Cruelest Month.* It is a retrograde step, and will more than likely cause the critics to make all of the classic remarks usually said about second novels. It is not a good book; in fact, it is so bad that it is difficult, if not impossible, to take seriously.

Once inside this book you may feel like a gambler in a strange town running about and crying plaintively, "Where's the action?" About two thirds of it is talk. All of a Henry

From "Sound and Fury," a review by Robert Harlow. In *Canadian Literature* 19 (Winter 1964), pp. 58-59. By permission of Robert Harlow.

Green book is talk—talk such as you've never heard before. Mr. Buckler's book is talk which you've heard many times before—not from the mouths of human beings, but from the pens of bad writers who think they are depicting sophisticated people saying sophisticated things. Huxley managed it, I suppose, and Norman Douglas in *South Wind;* Ronald Firbank could do it and make it seem very real in an oddly rococo way. But Mr. Buckler's talkers are very unreal because they only talk about themselves, or more impossibly, about something that interests the author. They not only talk themselves, but they try to get each other to talk. The central third of the novel is comprised of chapters where a half-dozen characters are paired off and each breaks down the other's reserve and reticence and makes him talk. A forty-year-old spinster and a fifty-year-old thrice-wed Robert Ruark-type novelist talk themselves into marriage; a medical student and a young New York matron talk themselves into listening to the wild sexual call of their autonomic nervous systems; and in the end, Paul, the hero, one supposes, talks himself into falling in love with Letty, the illiterate housekeeper widow who opines that "all the readin' and writin' that was ever done" (at Paul's place) "wouldn't amount to a fart on the plains of Arabia." It is difficult not to like her. She speaks eloquently for the reader.

Paul runs a kind of hotel, which is a haven for intellectuals, called Endlaw, which is twenty miles from Granfort, which is a fair day's drive from Halifax, which is a naval base on the Atlantic seaboard of Canada. Besides Paul, who has learned that if you jolly people along and look mysterious you will in fact *be* mysterious, there is Letty, grotesque because the author thinks of her as such, and Kate, who really loves Paul but who becomes engaged to Morse who is a novelist who begins to write a novel about the characters at Endlaw Mr. Buckler is writing about, and Sheila who is rich and married to Rex who is tense about his lowly background and his spotty war record, and finally Bruce who is nurturing guilt because he was the instrument that killed his son and wife in a car accident. At the end of the book there is a forest ranger named Leander

Farquharson who interrupts a forest fire which is the best thing in the book by far. The reason, I think, is that it is very active and doesn't have a word to say about how to write a novel, or about Life or Love or Relationships that Must Be. Another thing about the forest fire is that it is unpredictable. Without a word it jumps the creek everybody says it coudn't. It also gets Letty's skirt off her, gives Paul a heart attack, separates all of the sexual sheep from their intellectual wolves' clothing, and does it by just going about its real business, which is to ignite and burn down as much timber as it possibly can before it gets rained on. I wonder if there isn't a lesson in that for novelists like Mr. Buckler.

What he has done—with more sweat and toil that I care to think about—is to write 298 pages of notes on what could be a story of more than a little interest. They are the kind of notes that are perhaps necessary to a good novel, but once written down they should be abandoned and used, as the memory of actual experience is sometimes used to colour our speculation about experiences yet to come. It is enough for the author to remember that Paul is the kind of selfish-little-boy-god who would find a mate in Letty. It is too much for the story to have him actually do it. It is enough for Mr. Buckler to know that Morse would subject a group of people to a game of Truth. It is embarrassing to have him do it. Actually, the most successful character in the book is Rex. He is object rather than subject. He is simply viewed by the others and he acts from real tensions that he does not understand. He is consistent in his gratuitousness from birth to the moment of his triumph when he has his wife Sheila trapped and he flips away the cigarette butt that starts the forest fire. After I had closed the book I wondered about Rex. The others I was simply glad to be done with.

Mr. Buckler can use language well. Many times in the book you will be dragged into a paragraph and pushed out again with your imagination tingling with the rightness of his image or his way with words. But he suspends animation. This book is a still-life with sound track.

3. CONNECTION OF CHARACTER AND PLACE

JACK SHERIFF

Some of the most memorable novels that I have read—and these happen to be "Canadian"—include *The Double Hook, The Sacrifice, Execution, The Rich Man, Who Has Seen the Wind, Judith Hearne,* and *The Mountain and the Valley* (the last by Ernest Buckler). *The Cruelest Month,* Buckler's second novel, certainly belongs in this listing.

Very little actually happens in *The Cruelest Month,* and yet one becomes completely absorbed by the mental actions and reactions of the seven principal characters whose physical and spiritual paths criss-cross in a most dramatic fashion. Hardly a word is wasted by this most economic writer; indeed, occurrences and thoughts are fraught with connotation.

Claude Bissell describes Buckler's use of events in *The Mountain and the Valley* as follows: "What he does is to select an event and then explore in great detail the emotional results, as if he threw a small pebble into a pool and then charted the ripples that arise, spread outward, and finally break on the shore." In *The Cruelest Month,* instead of treating the various events in one person's life, Buckler has concentrated on the single event of bringing several people from various backgrounds together at a Nova Scotian country guesthouse called Endlaw, and allowing us to observe the relationships that form. In many ways, Buckler's work reminds one of E. M. Forster, whose primary concern is with character and with personal relationships ("only connect" being the guiding principle underlying *Howards End*). The importance of *place* as well as persons is another similarity between the two writers. Buckler begins his novel by quickly establishing the setting for the personal drama that is to be enacted.

At first glance, Paul's place was no more than a small, white, friend-faced house standing beside a lake still as theorems.

From "New Novel Reviewed," by Jack Sheriff. In *Amethyst* 3 (Winter 1964), pp. 54-56. By permission of Jack Sheriff.

Someone else's snapshot. And then you saw what was perfect about it. Simple though it was, and chanced together though it had been by builders who as architects were total innocents, it had the inevitability of a master painting.

The elements of fire and water likewise play their part. Following the purging fire of man and nature that serves as a physical climax to the novel, the rain's restorative effects are soon felt. "The rain had brought out the first *thick* sigh of green on everything; and tree and bush stood as stuporously-dotingly delivered of their leaves as animals of their young," symbolising the "connecting" that is taking place in man circumscribed by his environment.

Buckler does not so much view his characters; rather he lets the reader see each character's view of himself. This is accomplished by the character in isolation, in relation to family or friends, in terms of time-past, -present and -future, and finally in reaction to a developing or already-developed love. Eventually, as a result of an abrupt awakening, each character re-evaluates and reassesses himself, and his relationships. One could almost apply the Hegelian dialectic of *thesis*, *antithesis*, and *synthesis* as the informing pattern of the novel.

Bruce Mansfield deserts his ambition to be a doctor because of a past haunted by the accidental death of his wife and child for which he blames himself. A love affair with Sheila Giorno helps him to forget until she breaks with him to remain with her husband. Somehow, however, the whole experience reconciles him to the past and simultaneously frees him.

Bruce turned toward Halifax. The hills and valleys of his senses were suddenly levelled when Sheila turned the other way. His consciousness took the imprint of the letters on the corner billboard like a *tabula rasa*. GRANFORT—FOUNDED 1782. Every single soul living in the world then was dead now. Dead —Gone. Live—Love—Lose. Ago—Ago—The memory of Sheila's face stamped the word "ago" across everything.

Similarly with Morse, Sheila, Rex, Paul, Kate and Letty, each undergoes a baptism of sorts. For Kate, the ordeal is by fire. "Her lips were speechless with trembling, but in every limb of her mind she felt a strange new firmness. As if fire had tempered her." Oddly, the central crisis is created by ineffectual, self-crippled Rex Giorno whose two badly-managed "accidents" of an apparent suicidal attempt and the ill-considered dropping of a lighted cigarette are the catalysts that cause reevaluation and lead to readjustment.

The character relationships at the close of the novel are not predictable: Shelia and Rex remain together; Kate and Morse get together; Bruce Mansfield has come to terms with his dead wife and child; and Paul will "connect" with the unlikely Letty, and thereby find release and safety even from the Damocles sword of a bad heart ("And in the moment when his flesh was exquisitely pitted of its stone, he had a glimpse of Death's losing face dissolving far far behind. . . .")

E. K. Brown, in his excellent book *Rhythm in the Novel,* describes the structure of E. M. Forster's *A Passage to India* as having a "rhythmic rise-fall-rise." *The Cruelest Month* appears to have this general sort of structure, and perhaps it is just such a pattern that allows Buckler the scope he needs for his brilliant analysis of individual character.

The Cruelest Month is high on my list of recommended reading—and bears rereading.

---

4. CREED AND CRAFT EXPOUNDED

R. G. BALDWIN

Few reviewers will risk a prose flourish at the expense of this painfully honest book. Buckler will have the skin off anyone who goes for an easy mark, anyone, including himself. A neurotic perfectionist, he worries and fidgets a handful of disenchanted but highly intelligent people into precisely the required positions for psychic surgery, and then spends the rest of his time readjusting those positions. The result is brilliant

From a review of *The Cruelest Month,* by R. G. Baldwin. In *Queen's Quarterly* 71 (Summer 1964), p. 277. By permission of R. G. Baldwin.

but exhausting. One of his characters almost says it: "All that bloody sweat over blokes that come out sounding as if they needed to be wormed."

And yet that is unfair, as almost any comment on this book must be, because nothing can be said to Buckler that would not be asking him to sell out. For better or worse, this is his book, and the incredible pains he takes to pin down exactly the mood of the moment suggest that he could not have written it in any other way. Here is a man giving everything he has. The trouble is he tries to give more—at least in his style, which is sometimes grotesquely difficult, almost self-consuming as it turns in on itself. When his people talk, the dialogue can leap and crackle. But when he subjects them to analysis he makes the most frightful demands on himself (and his reader): "He caught himself close to the wispily elegiac plaintiveness that unconsciously poeticizes itself, frighteningly close to rehearsing his deprivation with that toxic 'lingering' regard of the self-commiserative."

His characters do, however, get born of the talk, thoroughly born, though labour is protracted and delivery takes very nearly two-thirds of the book. On the whole, they are worth waiting for, especially Morse, the self-conscious novelist who, in expounding his creed, tells us more about the writer's craft than most anthologies on the subject. If Buckler ever gets to the point of being fair game for "studies," this book will be a godsend to the scholars undertaking them, for the creed expounded is obviously Buckler's own, and the book discussed by his novel-writing character is, just as obviously, this one.

The reader who stays with it will be rewarded by the many times when book takes strongly over from author and, like a current momentarily breaking free from obstructions, leaps to vigorous and exciting life. But do not stay with it quite to the end. For there, incredibly after what has gone before, Buckler decides he has had his fill of characterizing people by their troubles and that it is time for April to give way to May. Until then the cruelest month is chronicaled by a writer of great, if unresolved, power.

5. THE PRICE OF DETACHMENT AND INDEPENDENCE

F. W. WATT

The rest of this year's books answer the usual expectations: these are mainly works of contemplative realism and historical romance. In many ways the most impressive of those which remain to be discussed is almost an epitome of the best and worst features of Canadian fiction: Ernest Buckler's long overdue second novel, *The Cruelest Month*. Here is intelligence, thoughtfulness, and sincerity, and here too is an extraordinary awkwardness and heaviness. Buckler is the most difficult kind of novelist to assess fairly—conventional and often clumsy enough in technique to tempt an easy dismissal, but possessed of a meditative purposefulness which draws one willy-nilly into the lives and thoughts of his characters and into the never entirely convincing world they inhabit.

The chief failure of the novel is that the author tells us about his characters, giving a set of intelligent, complex case-histories of potentially interesting people, and they talk endlessly about themselves and each other, but they are never really shown, presented, brought alive. Buckler's stylistic mannerisms and preciousness are no doubt called forth by a need to raise, intensify or gain immediacy for what is basically a non-dramatic imagination. In dialogue all the characters alike speak in contrived figures of speech, creating a veritable graveyard of dead metaphors and similes. (They all have, incidentally, the same taste for mildly scatological humour, perhaps the least amusing feature of the book.) In narration the author resorts to double-barrelled volleys—"wonder-struck," "spell-caught," "friend-faced," "proudly-foolishly," "flesh-substantialed," "strangely-instantaneously," "tremor-music," and so on.

The least laboured and most effective part of the novel is the story of Paul, the middle-aged reclusive farmer and resort

From "Letters in Canada: 1963—Fiction," by F. W. Watt. In *The University of Toronto Quarterly* 33 (1964), pp. 396-97. By permission of F. W. Watt.

keeper whose country house, Endlaw (an anagram for Walden) provides the main setting. Paul's belated discovery of the price he has paid for his lifelong poise, detachment and independence —to die, as he will soon from heart failure, knowing that he has never moved within the doorways of another human spirit —is depicted with a genuine moving force. There is a certain force to the conclusion, also, though it risks banality, which shows Paul turning with surprised relief from the complex, sophisticated, intellectualized love of one woman to the crude, ordinary, taciturn, long-lived loyalty of another: "He felt beautifully simple, and she was the beautiful monosyllable of home." But the intertwined lives of the handful of guests who have come to rest and find themselves in Paul's Thoreauesque retreat are by comparison unconvincing and inert. The spectacular and splendidly described forest fire that ends the book, with its purgatorial and tempering flames, comes not a moment too soon to remind us that the author of *The Mountain and the Valley* has a powerful imagination, however cramped and inhibited it too often is.

THE WAY IT WAS

D. O. SPETTIGUE

Canadian literature seems to have come into existence at an opportune time for the student of English-Canadian prose. Two articles that have appeared in this quarterly, Warren Tallman's "Wolf in the Snow" and D. G. Jones's "The Sleeping Giant," have set a new standard of imaginative criticism of the novel. It may now be possible to examine the English-Canadian novel within a conceptual framework whose terms are supranational but whose application is readily adjusted to the national scene. Ernest Buckler is one author whose work lends itself to such treatment.

The two studies already mentioned show the influence of Northrop Frye and Roy Daniells. Roy Daniells has been foremost among those critics who have looked to the accidents of geography and climate for an explanation of certain characteristics of English-Canadian fiction. His assessment of the role of the "terrain," and Northrop Frye's identifying of fear and the "garrison mentality" as characteristic attitudes in our prose, are the more generalized precursors of the "Wolf in the Snow" and "Sleeping Giant" studies. W. R. Wilgar's "Poetry and the Divided Mind," to which Mr. Jones refers, is another parent of what may be called the "between two worlds" theme recognized by recent critics.

If it has been difficult in the past for critics to find a conceptual framework in which to treat English-Canadian fiction, that is partly because the writers have had such difficulty in finding a focus themselves. They have therefore tended to look to the past for the illusions of unity or order, or abroad to

"The Way It Was," by D. O. Spettigue. In *Canadian Literature* 32 (Spring 1967), pp. 40-56. By permission of D. O. Spettigue.

greener pastures than a raw colony could offer. Among the early writers Major Richardson depicts British redcoats beseiged in their forts in a wilderness connotative of fear. Mrs. Moodie, during the seven years in the bush clearing that she calls a "prison-house," looks to England as "home," but exhorts Canadians to work for their country's growth. Haliburton is another who contrasts the dismal present with what Maritime Canada could become. E. W. Thomson creates a Loyalist who, facing death by drowning, is content as long as he drowns on the Canadian side of the river. The inhabitants of Scott's Viger are trapped by their environment, but those in his northern tales are a part of the landscape. Modern English-Canadian writers renew the imagery of the threatening terrain, notably Sinclair Ross and Sheila Watson, but Malcolm Lowry finds in Canada both rest and inspiration, and Hugh MacLennan's Odysseyan heroes, singing its vastness, seek themselves in seeking the source of its nationhood.

With nearly two centuries of fiction behind us it is possible to identify, somewhat more nearly than Mr. Jones has done, the Edenic image in our fiction as the environment of childhood or the immediate vanishing past, and to relate both Frye's "tone of deep terror in regard to nature" and Jones's Sleeping Giant to the perpetuation of the settler's response to the British North American terrain. The recurrent phrase, "the way it was," in Ernest Buckler's fiction is then relatable to the three fundamental attitudes to the Canadian environment, as *threat* (the wolf-in-the-snow or exiles-from-the-garden or drowned-poet or buried-life theme), as *haven* (the Canaan or New-World or Promised-Land theme) and as *potential* (the Adam-about-to-awake or child-of-nations-giant-limbed theme).

Ernest Buckler has been publishing fiction for some twenty-five years but, although he began his writing career with a prize-winning article and won the *Maclean's* fiction award in 1948, it was only with *The Mountain and the Valley* (1952) that he won critical attention. Again, he won the President's Medal for the best Canadian short story in both 1957 and 1958, but it was the publication in 1961 of the New Canadian Library edition of *The Mountain and the Valley* that won a wide audience for the retired philosopher of Bridgetown, Nova Scotia.

Writer of poetry, newsletters, articles, CBC scripts, novels and short stories, Buckler nevertheless has come to be known as the author of one novel. The phenomenon of the novelist who publishes one promising book and then sinks into silence, or who after many a summer publishes a second that does not seem to fulfil the promise of the first, is almost a Canadian tradition. It could therefore be predicted that Buckler's second novel, *The Cruelest Month* (1963), would excite less comment than the first. It could also be predicted that the second novel would be less obviously confessional. But Buckler is already advanced in a third novel, and seems quite uninterested in conforming to expectation. One might even guess that he does not much care about the patterns of English-Canadian fiction. He knows what his fellows are doing but, like them, if he reads fiction at all it is likely to be contemporary American or European. It may then be asked whether there is any need to stress the Canadianism of an author who, unlike, say, Hugh MacLennan, does not take the national approach. The reply must be that there are distinct patterns in English-Canadian fiction which are just now coming to be recognized and that Buckler's fiction, which seems not only to conform to but almost to epitomize them, is worth studying as part of that context. A second reply is that, despite the obvious dangers and limitations of parochialism, it is no disadvantage, when judging the national product in the international arena, to know what the national product is.

"The way it was," or "how it was," occurs as commonly in Buckler's short stories and articles as in his novels. "How can you tell," he asks in the reminiscent article "School and Me," "such things as how it was the morning the mote-thickened spring sunshine slanted through the open window and you saw that the figure you were dividing with was the same figure in the denominator of the answer . . .?" In "The Clumsy One," a short story very close to the style of *The Mountain and the Valley,* the narrator broods: "I had the quicker way with the mind, and still I couldn't feel how it was with him, the way he seemed to know, with a quiet sensing, exactly how it was with me." The story "The Quarrel," which won the *Maclean's* prize for 1948, is built on a series of contrasts between the way a boy had expected the day of the fair to be, and the way it actually was: "That's exactly how it turned out to be . . . You see, that was the August Sunday which was to have been twice as wonderful . . . But it wasn't like other mornings . . . We didn't keep saying what a perfect day it was . . . ." And at the climax: "Now here is where I wish for the subtlety to show you, by the light of some single penetrating phrase, how it was driving home. But I can only hope that you will know how it was, from some experience of your own that was sometime a little like it."

Roy Daniells is one of many critics to comment on the prominence in English-Canadian prose fiction of reminiscence, especially of childhood scenes set on the farm or in the village and attempting to capture the flavour of a way of life that can no longer be the way it was. The rural idyll of the late nineteenth and early twentieth centuries was a sentimental development of that characteristic. Grove, Knister, Connor, Slater and W. O. Mitchell have exploited such material in sustained works, and it has been the staple of the short stories and sketches that make up so much of our prose tradition.

The Buckler short stories date from two *Esquire* publications of 1940/41, a promising year for Canadian fiction, though it must be admitted that the early stories showed little more than a facility with language. The published stories together seem to divide into four quite distinct groups. The *Saturday Night* group of the war years have a Sunday-school sentimentality about them, but introduce the concern with guilt, at any kind of separation or alienation, until separateness is resolved in a moment of transfiguring unity. The second group chronologically are the *Maclean's* stories of 1948 to 1951, which include Buckler's best: "Penny in the Dust," "The Quarrel," "The Clumsy One" and "The Rebellion of Young David." To these should be added "The Wild Goose" from the *Atlantic Advocate*, in which he has continued to publish to the present. These five stories are similar in style, theme and characterization to *The Mountain and the Valley* and might be considered exercises toward that novel, except that "The Rebellion of Young David" is incorporated in *The Cruelest Month*. The *Atlantic Advocate* group is generally less impressive but includes a number of stories exploring the personal and professional frustrations of the writer in his search for the unifying vision. These are suggestive of *The Cruelest Month* and again explore some of its specific complex relationships. Two stories from *Chatelaine* of 1956 and 1957 extend the *Mountain and the Valley* material. The remaining stories form a group of some range, from humour to thriller, but without much enlargement of the reader's experience.

Like the best of the stories, the two novels are set in the Annapolis Valley area of Nova Scotia. The principal difference between them is in range of characterization and time span. The first novel is a story of childhood and adolescence within a closely knit family group, but it is framed by a Prologue and an Epilogue set just before the protagonist's death, to which all the past has contributed. The action of the second novel occupies only a few days, with generous portions of flashback, but only the interpolated story reaches back into the rural past of *The Mountain and the Valley*. Like the [first] novel, it is intensely involved in the complexities of hurting and healing in the context of love.

The representative Buckler activity is reminiscing, the area of reminiscence is characteristically the childhood environment, and the emotions recurrently evoked are those of contrasting gloom and joy. The "it" of "the way it was" is the meanest of terms but on it is placed the burden of conveying the most transcendent experiences of unity in the fleeting moment. Against the memories of ecstatic experiences of wholeness are set those of separation, dissolution and alienation, and these are associated with guilt at the failure to seize the offered moment in which harmony might have been restored. The "was" of the phrase thus represents a complex of times in which the moment being lived by the character is contrasted with an ideal might-have-been which in turn is extracted from the recollection of an actual "was" of the character's past. That recalled moment (often the climax for which the suspenseful preparation is also given, as the days and hours leading to a child's Christmas) can only be rendered in terms of sense impressions—the way someone's face looked, what colour the leaves took in a certain light, how a voice would sound, the way the spring earth smelled, the feel of new skates, the warmth of familiar things— all intensely realized. At the same time, one is aware of an opposite impression, that these novels are remarkably abstract. Even in the sensuous *The Mountain and the Valley* the language may be that of the withdrawn intelligence extracting the essence of familial relations in analogies almost geometrically balanced. A balance in tension is created by comparing the present situation with a past or hypothetical situation which, if it obtained now, would reverse the present. But the perversities of human nature wilfully distort emotion, preventing communication, until just the right combination of sense impressions and circumstance bursts the floodgates of remorse and longing, restores unity and duplicates in the present the desirable emotion of the past.

This is a language of simile—not what *is,* but what it is *like.* The basis of the similes is the division of personality which can find analogies in two contrasting kinds of scenes, those of unity and those of discord. The basis of this division, in turn, is the divided personality, which has its counterpart in the divisions of the book.

The novel divides into six parts with Prologue and Epilogue, the eight parts tending to resolve themselves into two sequences. The first, the Prologue and Parts One to Three, are feminine in orientation; they are of the Valley. Parts Four to Six, the second sequence, are masculine; they align with the Epilogue, "The Mountain." In his Introduction to the New Canadian Library edition, Claude Bissell compares *The Mountain and the Valley* to "Fern Hill" as "a magnificent paean to the wonder and innocence of youth." The comparison is applied to the first half of the book only, for "the very strength and sureness of Buckler's treatment of the family . . . makes the last section of the book something of an anticlimax." This is to overlook the structural unity of David's struggle with time. The focus of the first half is forward; David's responses to praise, to shame and to love, and his anticipation of the revenge or repayment or glory that he knows some day will be his. It is this sequence that has all the wonder, the enthusiasm and beauty of awakening youth. But the seeds of destruction are there. For all David's love of family and farm home, he is an alien spirit. In a magnificently rendered scene at the centre of the novel, his frustration breaks out in a quarrel with his father. With the cruel desire to hurt and to escape, David provokes his father to a blow, then flees from home. But on the road to the city he is haunted and overwhelmed by the recalled faces of home, and he turns back.

He came to the bridge. He could see the house again. The ash of the quarrel, of blows given and felt, was tamped down physically into his flesh. The soreness was drawn out wire-thin, pendant at the corners of his lips. Suddenly he put his head into the only place left to hide: the crook of his elbow along the rail of the bridge. He began to sob. He sobbed because he could neither leave or stay. He sobbed because he was neither one thing nor the other.

The chapter ends with his grandmother giving David the locket containing the photo of the sailor she once had hidden in the barn—symbol of the restless adventuring spirit she still supposes David will be. David is puzzled by the gift.

And then suddenly he knew where he'd seen a face like that. He was looking at it right there in the mirror. This locket had something to do with what had happened today. She'd sensed somehow what had happened. She'd sensed it because she too knew what it was like when the moonlight was on the fields when the hay was first cut and you stepped outside and it was lovely, but like a mocking—like everything was somewhere else.

He went to sleep at once, though. He was eighteen.

At this point David still is young enough to look forward

to achievement and happiness. But by the end of Part Five, with Joseph's death, the watershed has been crossed. Hereafter the bright moments will exist only in memory. "It would seem as if everything had gone by while he slept, down the road, and now he'd never catch up with it."

In the second sequence the family unity that had provided the vitality begins to crumble; disintegration marks the central parts of the book, and thereafter the focus is backward as David declines into a defensive routine and withdraws even from the limited local society. This is the "buried life," the "ritual death" from which David must resurrect himself. The means to freedom is his discovery of his potential for writing. His childhood sensitivity to the familiar surroundings, and the anonymity that had enabled him to become the voice for others and release their tensions in ribaldry, now enable him to record with increasing precision "the way it is" at certain moments of the rural day. Like a new Adam, he will conquer his environment by naming it. The environment itself has thus changed from threat to potential, and now contains within itself the possible resolution of David's conflicting desires.

The title, *The Mountain and the Valley,* draws attention to the principal organizing device, the series of related, usually contrasting or complementary, symbols. The book is "about" the achieving of unity in an environment that does not seem to encourage unity—and thus the relation between Buckler and the Canadian prose tradition. The eight images named in the titles of the Prologue, Epilogue and the six Parts of the book are all indicative of the attempts, successful and unsuccessful, at reconciliation. "The Mountain" and "The Valley" make one complementary pair. They relate to certain characters and principles, as Mountain *vs.* Valley, Father *vs.* Mother, Male *vs.* Female, Toby *vs.* Anna, the tall pine *vs.* the house or, since the pine is to be the keel for a boat, the Ark (in Mr. Jones's terms) *vs.* the farm or garden. As in D. H. Lawrence, male and female are in opposition, antagonisms flaring or settling dully in at a word misinterpreted, a jealousy mistakenly aroused. Anna can find her fulfilment only through Toby, yet the two know very few moments of peace in their short life together. Chris, David's older brother (here, as in "The Clumsy One" and "The Wild Goose" the slow, inarticulate but intuitively knowing one, the one who belongs to the country) is forced by the demands of young sexuality into a marriage and a house where there is neither love nor understanding, where only separation can follow. David's early love is the pathetic Effie, a foil for the Anna David would marry were she not his sister. (Toby, whom she does marry, is virtually a double of David.) David tries to demonstrate a sexual prowess at Effie's expense and for Toby's benefit, but fails. Perhaps a kind of unity could be achieved in a sexual union wherein both accomplishment and security might be found, as in *The Cruelest Month*. But there is no such love outside his parents' marriage—this is precisely David's problem on one level. The climax of Part One is David's participation with Effie in a school play. Like a younger Stephen Dedalus, he dreads and somewhat despises the gross event, but finds the play becoming a unity and achieving an effect beyond the worth of the parts or the players. This is the only promise David is given of a potential harmony that is not simply the effects of natural phenomena operating on youthful sensitivity. But a total unity is not achieved. David lacks Stephen's awareness of the distinction between the artifice and the fact; when he tries to kiss his startled princess and a coarse voice shouts applause, stepladder and Effie and illusion crash to the floor, and David flees. The play, first symbol in the first sequence, does not point the way to a resolution.

The second symbol, for which Part Two is named, is the Letter. Via a pen club, David makes contact with Toby who will become his only friend. That is, he has communicated with the outside world. Toby is a second David—in one scene David admires himself in Toby's sailor cap and realizes he could be Toby—just as both Toby and David are associated with the half-mythical sailor old Ellen had once hidden in her barn. He is the symbol of the restless spirit, the questing, moving male by contrast with the waiting female. After their marriage, Anna and Toby are separated most of the time, he away on naval duty, she awaiting his occasional returns. When he is lost at sea, she does not return to the farm. She has chosen the outside world and cannot go home again. Toby and Anna, then, are the questing side of David, and with their loss he is doomed to stagnate at home.

In the second sequence the equivalent communication to the Letter is the Train of Part Six. As so often in North American fiction, the train is the means to escape into the larger world— it has this role in Sinclair Ross's *As For Me and My House* and *The Well*. In the last leave-taking with Toby, David goes to the front field to watch Toby wave from the train. Toby, absorbed in another world with other friends, does not even look. David goes berserk, hacking in impotent fury at the parsnips that are rooted like him, the half-self that will never enlarge itself again, "because all the crossroad junctions had been left irretrievably far behind."

Balancing Part One, the Play, is Part Five, the Scar. During the killing and scalding of a pig (another of Buckler's wonderfully exact scenes of farm life), David falls from a rafter and sustains a permanent injury and scar. Thereafter the pain is part of his consciousness, leaving him only in rare moments of renewed hope. The fall and scar would link David with the Adam and wounded god figures of mythology, while his weak heart makes his exile from the vital life a permanent condition, the state of man.

The Prologue and the Epilogue, entitled "The Rug" and "The Mountain," are the other complementary parts. Once David has discovered that he can write, his ingrown self can be freed into anonymity by becoming the myriad elements of its environment and then be expressed in words. Only then can the Sleeping Giant wake, the wounded god be resurrected, the Word recreate the Flesh. But mastery of words is a potential only. David's environment provides him with a stimulating flux; it does not provide the models of harmony that he needs for literary form, and his potential book is therefore never written. He is frustrated by sheer quantity of impression. The challenge his environment offers him is to create the intelligible order of literature from what might be called an "unintelligible land-scape." He tries to acknowledge each component individually and of course is overwhelmed. What he lacks is the abstracting power of symbol, the kind of pattern his grandmother weaves out of experience.

The Epilogue continues the Prologue, both occurring in the same afternoon and developing the same few phrases. Here old Ellen has something of the role of Lily Briscoe of *To the Lighthouse,* her rug pattern developing parallel to the action and completing itself as the action is completed, so that one unity is accomplished, that of the family in the context of cyclical time. In the Prologue David stands at the window—a telling Canadian position—while behind him his grandmother selects her rags and weaves them into her rug. In the Epilogue David flees this house of death and bondage and climbs the mountain of his lifelong desire, while Ellen continues with her rug.

As he ascends, David goes through the nightmare of guilt at all the creation he has failed to name. No longer recalling, he is reliving all the significant moments of his past that cry out accusingly for expression. He is seeing, hearing, feeling not only the present sensations but all those of his past. Under the pressure of accumulated sensation David achieves a moment of mystical exaltation, "The complete translation to another time" which Buckler celebrates and represents. "It is not a *memory* of that time," for "the years between have been shed." The im-mediate becomes the past and "there is an original glow on the faces like on the objects of home." But David's exultation be-comes horror as he tries to respond to all the demanding past in the present as well as the swarming present itself: "That little cloud that way and no other; that little cloud I didn't see, ex-actly the way *it* was," and so with the way everything has been and will be, and even might have been, all pursuing him "with the relentless challenge of exactly how each one was," until in horror he "put his arms about the great pine and thrust his forehead against its hard body," screaming "Stop." With this strong masculine image his nightmare ceases. He has reached the top of the mountain and has ended his purgatory with the sudden conviction that he can *become,* and thereby encompass and control, all those demanding experiences. Adam will become his universe in naming it: "I know how it is with everything. I will put it down and they will see that I know." Then the blackness that is the outer border of Ellen's rug "swam in his head again," turns grey, then the white of the centre of her rug, and David, dead, is buried in snow. But the unity of mountain and valley is completed as a partridge flies from the mountain to the valley in a single direct movement that recalls the single brush stroke with which Lily Briscoe completed her painting and achieved the unity of the lighthouse. At this same moment Ellen has completed her rug and has shown her way to unity, as she sorts through the clothing of the living and the dead to weave into her rug. She lets selected objects include and stand for the multiplicity of associations as one coloured rag in her rug is both the focus of all associations of its relation to its onetime wearer, and also a part in the design of the rug that includes those associations but recreates them in a significant order. The concentric circles of coloured clothing in the rug expand from a point of white, as David's consciousness struggles against the nightmare of expanding detail, only to contract again sharply to the point of [white] lace and the snowflakes which are, in terms of the novel, the achieved unity, and in terms of David's potential, the irony of another buried life.

David Canaan's literary family is a prominent one in English-Canadian fiction. There was the ancestral Mrs. Moodie at midcentury, warning that this land of promise was a "prison-house" for the educated until the prosaic arts of nation-building had been accomplished. There was Grove's Len Sterner at the turn of the century, still pioneering, frustrated and defeated by poverty because the physical accomplishment that would free the intellect from material necessity had still not been realized, perhaps could not be realized where nature without conspired with nature within to distract a youth from the very struggle it imposed upon him. There was Knister's Richard Milne carrying on a forlorn courtship with the ingrown spirit of rural Ontario, as David with the Annapolis Valley. But Richard had a road out; for David, the trains run everlastingly away. Among the moderns there is Robertson Davies' Monica Gall, who lacks even the awareness of potential until accident provides the money—the only gift of her environment—for an escape out of Canada and into fulfilment. Finally there is Sinclair Ross's Philip Bentley perpetuating the spirit of Horizon by preaching a creed he no longer believes in, until self-pity and the promptings of sex, sole agents of revolt in such a climate, impel him to flee to the city, where a human community may be found sufficient to create the necessary illusion of stability. And then there is David, for whom the green and golden promise of the Annapolis Valley seen through the eyes of youth fades into the light not only of common day but of sterility absolute. Where Sinclair Ross achieves the effects of monotony in order to render the failure of creativity from lack of stimulation, Ernest Buckler achieves the effects of redundance in order to render the failure of creativity from lack of focus.

Like many another confessional writer of the modern mode, Mr. Buckler is concerned with the problems of the literary artist. He is one who can master words, who can bring to life the way an intense experience was; he has the language of the earth and the home, and the language of the flesh, as no other Canadian writer has them. And yet he distrusts words. He shows with surprising earnestness that distrust that is so profound in North American life—and that perhaps most definitely marks it off from Europe—of whatever savours too much of the study. This bias in Canadian fiction may help to account for its fondness for the pathos of the inarticulate victim, the stories of children and the animal story.

In *The Cruelest Month,* Letty is illiterate. In *The Mountain and the Valley* it is said of Chris that his thoughts were not "word-shaped," though they were thoughts none the less, and one detects in David—perhaps in Buckler himself— that sense of guilt on the part of the very articulate person that an anti-intellectual society fosters, as though too great a facility with words implied a lightness of character; a kind of black magic clings to the rituals of words even yet. Inarticulateness is part of the simplicity of rural life; Joseph, Martha, Chris and Ellen are strong almost *because* their thoughts are not word-shaped.

In *The Mountain and the Valley* Buckler refers to the "original simplicity of rural people." He contrasts it with the "artificial complexity" of city people, at least of those who have not gone beyond complexity to simplicity again. In *The Cruelest Month* he examines city people whose complexities are word-shaped, whose pastime is finding the words for their own emotions.

Formally, however, *The Cruelest Month* has a simpler structure than *The Mountain and the Valley*. Paul Creed has an old house in rural Nova Scotia; Kate Fennison, Morse Halliday, Rex and Sheila Giorno gather there for a spring-and-summer retreat. (It has to be April for Wastelandic reasons, but one feels that this should be a summer holiday; the weather lacks the sheer miserableness of a Canadian spring, and the forest fire sequence, though made plausible, seems to fit a later season.) The other visitor is Bruce Mansfield, whose family once owned Paul's place. He works occasionally on Paul's land, and joins the group because of a sudden infatuation with Sheila. This is the familiar "frame-story" setting, or the pattern of a Shakespearean romantic comedy. The characters withdraw from society into a green world where old conventions are allowed to lapse, where new relationships are allowed to develop and the genius of the place so manipulates or simply permits the action that the characters return to their real world with a new knowledge of themselves as the curtain drops. In this case all the actors, obsessed by guilt and fear, have failed to fulfil themselves. But being sophisticates—a professor's daughter, a society girl and her husband, and a writer—they disguise their uncertainties under a varnish of words that is supposed to reveal them. Among these is set Bruce, whose condition of guilty withdrawal resembles theirs, but who is less wordy because he is native to the area; the enigmatic Paul whose few words are a more effective defence than their many words; and Letty, the middle-aged and illiterate housekeeper who knows "the months on the calendar . . . and the days of the week. And her own name . . . And Paul's . . . And the short words you lived by." Letty dotes on Paul, but has no part in his life with these sophisticates: "They were his kind. She is not."

But Letty is only partly right about this. Like David, Paul is between two worlds, the Annapolis Valley world and the distant city—it is the familiar Archibald Lampman position. But unlike David, Paul has known the city world. One of David's attributes was his capacity to live vicariously, to *know* "the way it was" with people and in situations he never had experienced himself. David can talk the city talk, but he feels the guilt of betrayal if he does so. When he says "It's immaterial" to Toby, he knows he has made a breach with his rural schoolmates that can never be healed; language becomes the stockade for a garrison of two. But Paul is a David who has "gone outside," has been a city sophisticate and now has returned to the home soil (as Buckler himself did in 1936). Here he can be one with the local people when he chooses, or can open his doors to city people at will.

The reader's attitude to Paul is likely to vacillate. Interpreted generously, he is sharing with a few of the world's misfits who can benefit by them the healing powers of Paul's place and of himself. But their adoration of him, which puts him beyond all criticism—he's the singlest damn person; you don't know anything *about* Paul but you feel you know him— suggests that he is to be less a character than a manipulator, a Prospero whose detachment is almost too clinical. Paul's place is nicknamed Endlaw, not only as an anagram of the Walden it does not resemble but also as the place where the absurd rituals of social life are to be set aside (or replaced by other rituals). The name Paul Creed—it is almost too apostolic— may indicate a rooted faith or certainty by contrast with the creedless visitors who themselves have dubbed Endlaw "The Home for Incroyables," which may also suggest their unreality. Kate says of Endlaw: "You know time. Anywhere else, you hear its meter ticking whether you're using it or not. Here, that meter's stopped." Paul calls it "the one pocket of the universe that nothing could ever turn inside out," but this is also ironical, since Paul and his visitors are to be turned inside out before the novel ends.

Kate has been here before, with the father to whom she had devoted her life. On his death Kate, now a rootless spinster, flees the image of herself she sees being prepared in the faces around her. Morse has also been here before; his successful novel, significantly called *Each in His Narrow Cell,* was written at Endlaw. Now that his art and his life have staled, he returns in the hope of renewing the inspiration. The married pair are Sheila, society girl who has not yet told her husband that her family has lost its money and she is pregnant, and Rex, her poor-orphan spouse, whose good looks and naiveté have got him a war medal and Sheila and nothing else. The odd-man-out is Bruce, the disinherited Adam of this demi-paradise, and sometime medical student whose guilt at causing the death of his wife and son in a car accident has made him a recluse. In a kind of Midsummer Night's Dream the relations between characters are rearranged in spite of them. Bruce and Sheila fall in love and move inexorably to a sexual union before an accident returns them to their first loves. Kate, desperate to be fulfilled as a woman, allows herself to love Morse while uneasily aware that Paul is her soul-mate. Morse, thrice-married, accepts Kate in the expectation that she will be different, and that he can teach her to be a woman. The probability is that they will become another Sheila and Rex on a more rarified plane, the wife too readily seeing through, and less and less patiently condoning, the male posturing. And Paul, who loves Kate, so steels himself against that temptation that he is slow to see the alternative.

Fugitives from self-deception and social ritual, now they enmesh themselves in the rituals of their truth-and-consequences games which dare the participants to find the words for their secret selves. For Sheila, the most guarded, this is a temptation. For Kate it is part of the excitement she seeks; and for Morse, the cryptic writer, it's all grist for the mill. For Paul it is perhaps the holiday stimulant he thinks he needs, since for all his easy intimacy he only "rents people," keeping himself and Endlaw inviolate through the other three seasons. The member of the party the others ignore as beneath them, Rex, must amuse himself at tinkering and target practice and blunderings in and out of the others' incomprehensible conversations. They treat him as a child—formally his is a counterpart to Bruce's son Peter—but he is also, Caliban-like, an unwitting agent of the action. The rifle he fires in practice later wounds him by accident after Sheila has told him of her wish for a divorce. The wounding, misinterpreted as attempted suicide, brings the remorseful Sheila back to him, so duplicating the success of his phony war wound and freeing Bruce for a return to his medical training. At the end Sheila has accepted her lot with Rex, and Kate and Morse have gone off to be married.

But the projected holiday at Endlaw is cut short. After his guests arrive Paul secretly travels to Montreal for diagnosis of a heart condition. As in *The Mountain and the Valley* there is a watershed between the forward and the backward focus, so Paul's drive to the hospital, glossed over with clowning, is "the first high point in the arc of dissolution." The anchor in the others' lives, he now loses his certainty and feels the necessity to make "the definitive statement of himself. In one single sentence," which was the way of their game at Endlaw. Dismissing Kate and his other talkative friends, he determines to live his last seasons alone. Baffled and hurt they leave, but they complete the process of self-knowledge as they go. As unwitting agent, Rex causes a forest fire that threatens Endlaw just after the last visitors have left. Morse and Kate must drive through the fire and so endure a purgatorial ordeal which also faces Paul and Letty who battle the flames to the very edge of the house. When Paul collapses Letty learns of his illness as he learns of his need of her. It is "not words" he wants, but the living flesh.

The controlling symbols of this novel are the fire, the gun and the wounding of the "king," the exile and quest of the characters, Endlaw itself, the opposition between the Word

and the Flesh (the sophisticated talk *vs.* Letty's wonderful
silent hands, Morse and Kate's tortured examination of the
marital relation *vs.* the simple act of Paul and Letty), and
Paul, whose heart condition is the tangible mark of time and
whose self in retreat is the human condition.

Ernest Buckler is a novelist, not a romancer, and yet certain characteristics of the prose romance are discernible in *The
Cruelest Month.* One is the convention, as old as the *Decam-
eron,* of the withdrawal into a microcosmic world out of society
and out of time. Another is the use of such archetypes as the
purging and refining fire and the sick heart. A third is the
tendency of the characters to melt into one another, a characteristic of Buckler's fiction as a whole. Thus the short story
"Doctor and Patient" plays ironically with a writer who feels
he should have been a doctor and a doctor who should have
been a writer. In *The Cruelest Month* Paul, anonymously un-
dergoing examination in a Montreal hospital, adopts the name
Bruce Halliday, from Bruce Mansfield and Morse Halliday.
Bruce has been and will again be the doctor-in-training; Morse
is the writer. Paul, who feels that the chosen name suits him,
is another Buckler character who would like to be both. But
in some sense he *is* both, and this accounts for his enigmatical
anonymity. The element in him that would like to be savage
author lives vicariously in Morse (who also is Kate's lover as
Paul would be), as the element that would be first Adam in
this garden of man is displaced in Bruce.

The range of style is greater in this novel. These are outside
people coming to the Valley and being altered by it; those of
the first novel were Valley people going from or staying in it.
And these people are talkers, so that a conscious cleverness,
like the conscious allusiveness, must be part of the style. If a
language of abstraction was part of *The Mountain and the
Valley,* it is more so here where abstraction is a way of
life: "And for the moment they felt that curious disembodiment,
almost to the point of seeing their own faces as physically
pinched, which people whose chief alacrities reside in thought's
analysis and feeling felt between peaks of engagement." Beside

this language of analysis belongs that of the characters assessing themselves and one another, as in the anecdote of Paul and the bees. A third language is Paul's own calculated irreverence—that most essential creative gift—in balance with the reverence for the infinite variety of the familiar recurrent patterns of existence. This latter makes part of that language of reminiscence that dominates *The Mountain and the Valley;* the chapter that was published separately as "The Rebellion of Young David" is of that sort. The novelist's problem in introducing his characters is resolved here by a shifting of point of view. Part One begins with the characters gathered at Endlaw at the end of their first summer there. Part Two jumps five years to show them individually in the circumstances that will bring them back to Endlaw, and then another few days to show them arriving. The chapters of reminiscence serve to fill the five-year gap as well as to justify the characters as they are to be now. Thus Bruce's reminiscent chapter deals with his son Peter; in Part Two, in the present, Peter and Molly, Bruce's wife, are both dead.

Time and place make up the essential grid of Buckler's novels. Together with the bridging of time goes the focusing of time by coincidental place, a device that recalls Virginia Woolf's Mrs. Dalloway. Bruce has returned to the family farm, now Endlaw, and is chopping wood there for Paul—symbolically he is defining boundaries. As each of the visitors approaches he hears or does not hear Bruce's axe, which thus serves to pinpoint place and time. It is also a device for irony, since the sound of the axe has a different meaning for each: Kate thinks it a happy sound, but Bruce is slashing at trees as David slashed at parsnips. Morse hears it and recalls boyhood in Minnesota. But, as in *The Mountain and the Valley,* it is not recall but reliving. Yet Morse's response includes the commentary that makes explicit the imagery of the fall from that state of innocence which axe and deer are to connote. (The deer appears later in the novel for both couples to see, with much the significance of Frost's "Two Look at Two".) The scene that Morse recalls resembles the mountain and orchard of *The Mountain and the Valley* and the imagery is just in its vein of multiple simile: "the axe more beautiful like swimming naked than the gun is beautiful like Christmas." Both the form of that equation—like himself, Buckler's characters have an eye for mathematical relations—and the choice of swimming naked and Christmas as criteria of the ecstatic moment are typical of Buckler's language of innocence. But the tree falls and Morse returns to the cynical author of the present: "and he's lost his clean beautiful axe somewhere . . . and his very breakfast food is shredded wit."

Here again the contrast is between a world of childhood which recurs now only fitfully to remind you of the way it was, and a present world which is a state of experience, of knowing. The criticism so often made of the younger generation—that it knows too much—is made by Buckler in "School and Me." It is an acknowledgement of the growing sophistication of an affluent society. But Grove made the same observation a generation earlier, and perhaps every generation makes it. The point is, for Canadian literature the here and now is the place of knowledge, and knowledge is the fruit of the archetypal fall. The person who knows can never be content with this environment, and can never escape it. One hears, in *The Cruelest Month,* echoes of *The Mountain and the Valley* in the images of the great good time and the great good place that were one's childhood in rural Canada—and one realizes that one is hearing them from generations of Canadian writers. In *The Mountain and the Valley* too there was a fall to mark the loss of that time and place, after which place becomes bondage and exile, and time the one inexorable fact. Endlaw in *The Cruelest Month* is the place where, for a season, the garden seems to be regained, but where in fact man must labour and must come again to knowledge. Those who return to the stream of time are returning to a slightly lower world, a world longer and farther exiled, but they return there renewed by their contact with the terrain and themselves. And Paul, who makes again David's choice for the Valley, choosing the female of the flesh and the familiar way it was, has only a wince for the female of knowledgeable word and the way it might have been:

She stressed it again. "Just as soon as you've *drank* your coffee—"

Paul winced.

And then he grinned.

For a moment the April morning seemed to preen itself in that faultlessness which so mocks the one alone. And in that moment they felt the one inimitable safety. That great, sweet, wonderful safety from the cry of things not understood, of things said and things not said, of things done and things not done, of what is near and what far-off, and the sound of time and the sound of time gone by . . . .

ALL THE LAYERS OF MEANING

ALDEN NOWLAN

To me, Ernest Buckler's *The Mountain and the Valley* is not only the best novel yet written by a Canadian, but one of the great novels of the English language.

In my opinion, Buckler is one of the great masters of the simile. Buckler's most powerful similes not only illustrate the universality of a situation, but also its uniqueness. No one since D. H. Lawrence has created similes that are at once so fresh and so true.

Like Lawrence also, he has the ability to convey all the layers of meaning in a seemingly casual incident. I'm thinking now of the scene in *The Mountain and the Valley* in which he achieves the astounding feat of illuminating an entire way of life through what is, superficially, a description of a man and a woman cutting up the carcass of a hog.

Yet the great writing in *The Mountain and the Valley* seldom nudges the reader in the ribs: the casual reader could experience the book's power without stopping to think how that power was achieved. Buckler is not, in *The Mountain and the Valley* at least, a writer who stands on his head or waves his arms to show he isn't holding on to the handlebars.

Certainly, he has weaknesses. But, as with all great writers, his weaknesses are generally exaggerations of his strength. Like everyone who tries to write well and truly, he sometimes tries too hard. Then, sometimes, the similes slip out of his hands.

But, then, if I were to say that Buckler was perfect, there wouldn't be any reason for either him or me to go on writing.

From a letter to Gregory M. Cook from Alden Nowlan. In "Ernest Buckler: His Creed and Craft," an unpublished Master's thesis, Department of English, Acadia University (May 1967), p. 286. By permission of Alden Nowlan.

MY THIRD BOOK

ERNEST BUCKLER

A book which aims to give a comprehensive picture, descriptive and analytical, of Nova Scotian village life as I witnessed it at the time of my childhood and alter, in the vicinity of historied Annapolis Royal. This way of life, with all its distinctive customs, institutions, values, tasks, recreations, idioms of speech and behaviour, atmospheres and textural variety, has now vanished forever. I should like to triangulate it, so to speak, within the mingling stream of heritage, material change and social mutation.

The form this book would take would not be that of clinical documentary. My approach would be nearer the novelistic, using fact, incident and character as the prism of theme. I should hope that the trenchant humour of certain of its characters (who might have sat for Leacock) would enliven the book as it lent such colour to the fabric of their days—but the book would not be the conventional exercise in rustic anecdote. Except as they were individualistic to a degree, these characters were not "characters" after the "quaint" or "cracker-barrel" stereotype. And however inchoate their expression sometimes was, they were as charged with depths and intricacies of thought and feeling as the more sophisticated. Even in the small cross-section of life they represented, every conceivable psychological mode and subtlety had its embodiment.

The book would include personal reminiscences, but I should try hard to keep it from being just another wispily elegiac excursion into the "happy valley" of childhood. The autobiographical elements would be restricted to a minor feature in the

From copy of typescript to Gregory M. Cook, by Ernest Buckler. In *Ernest Buckler*: *His Creed and Craft,* an unpublished Master's thesis, Department of English, Acadia University (May 1967), pp. 256-60. By permission of Ernest Buckler.

objective general portrait; that of a uniquely and provocatively faceted way of Canadian life which, to my knowledge, has never had anything like the adequate record I feel it deserves.

Such a book, of course, must stand or fall on the author's ability to catch the essence of time, place and human equation: and it is very hard to put forward one's "ideatum" of means toward this end without sounding nebulous or pretentious. But I have some reason to hope that I could do the subject justice, simply and effectively.

After the joists are up, the roof shingled over, etc., there still remains the inside work. At present I am engaged in some interstitial passages (the windows, as it were) which, in a kind of pointillist fashion, will, I hope, illuminate the core of person and place. That is, juxtaposed clusters of carefully selected and particularly allusive detail, solid or atmospheric (e.g., the variant shades of weather and season that were such a subtle determinant in so many situations), which will summon up their whole context; as well as brief representative conversations which will evoke entire constellations (it is to be hoped) of circumstance and feeling behind them.

Re: revision.

This I find the most exacting and time-consuming of all. Carefully as I do compose even the first draft, I still feel obliged to weigh and examine each and every sentence again and again, groom it to the best effect I can manage. And even when the book is "all down," basically, each section must then be reassessed *in the light of the whole*. Certain sections must be shifted from one placement to another for better coordination. Lopsided emphases must be corrected by lengthening this paragraph, shortening that. Joints must be better articulated, transition seams erased. From time to time, better ways of saying the same thing will suggest themselves and order the recasting of a passage. Later ideas, in the light of the whole, must be inserted; and earlier ones, if suspected of clashing with the whole, must be pondered and, if found guilty, excised or replaced. Characters may need an added development, relationships a further clarification. Etc.

FIVE REVIEWS OF *OX BELLS AND FIREFLIES* (1968)

1: RETURN TO INNOCENCE AND WONDER

CLAUDE BISSELL

Ernest Buckler's first novel, *The Mountain and the Valley,* published in 1952, was the finest first book of any Canadian writer of this generation. It was a subtle and beautiful study of a young boy's growth to adulthood, and a companion study of family and community in rural Nova Scotia fifty years ago.

The Cruelest Month, which came some ten years later, was less successful; Buckler could not make his sophisticated, urban characters live, and the style often had a desperate, intense quality, as if the author despaired of ever seizing his material. It was none the less an important book, and in the perspective of Buckler's full career will emerge more clearly.

But there can be no doubt about his latest book, *Ox Bells and Fireflies.* With the artist's sure intuition, Buckler has returned to the world of *The Mountain and the Valley.* He has now abandoned his attempt to write a conventionl novel; *Ox Bells and Fireflies* has no plot, no continuous narrative development, no fixed cast of interacting characters. What he has tried to do is to give the very feel and pressure of the life that he knew and loved before the commercial revolution destroyed the small, self-contained farm and banished forever the rural Eden.

The result is what he has described as a "fictional memoir" —memories that cluster about specific incidents or are interwoven with customs and institutions. The point of view in the book constantly changes. We begin with the recollections of a

"A Masterly Return to Innocence and Wonder," By Claude Bissell. In *The Globe Magazine,* Toronto, Nov. 9, 1968, p. 16. By permission of Claude Bissell.

small boy; we move into the mind of his father or mother; or we move out into the mind of a sympathetic observer who writes humorously and affectionately of the folkways and customs of the times.

This is a book in praise of innocence and of the simple life close to nature. Strangely enough, in this young and innocent country, this has not been a notable theme. In the United States the romantic movement during the first decade of the nineteenth century drew its real nourishment from this theme, and Thoreau wrote its classic. But in Canada nature was either alien, a terrible and ruthless antagonist who threatened our very existence, or a domestic British garden seen through the mists of filial piety. The nature in *Ox Bells and Fireflies* is neither alien force nor protected garden. It is the natural complement of man. In this world man and nature join in love and understanding.

In a sense this is a sentimental book. Buckler believes that the simple life of the country fifty years ago represents an ideal. Passionate Maritime regionalist that he is, I suspect he would argue that the ideal reached its highest form in a small area in the Annapolis Valley where he grew up. He also believes that the city separates and kills, and that the country joins and heals. But this is the commonplace side of his central myth; the other side is the existence in the memory of an imperishable beauty that despises time.

I listen to the brook, and my own flesh and I are such snug and laughing brothers that I know we are forever mingled with the sun's pulse (or the wind's or the rain's) and forever unconquerable.

Buckler's Eden is all the more real because it stands in the shadow of time and knowledge. Beside the island of happiness is the island of despair.

You look outside yourself and you see only the blindness of people moving no less blindly than things . . . There is a bleaching yawn of distance between the closest things.

In Buckler's village "time was neither before you nor behind you; you were exactly opposite the present moment." But in the desolate urban landscape of later years time turns into fragments, and life into despair at what had gone and fear of what is yet to come.

This is a book written with great intensity. Every word has been tested for its exact ring. There are occasional low key sections of relaxed narrative and easy humorous description, but for the most part the style is metaphysical—a rarity in the flat landscape of our prose. There is some overreaching, places where the words refuse to be twisted or bent to support the thought. But there are many triumphs, passages of great and poignant beauty.

In one place Buckler says of his rural people that "since birth they had seen the wind and heard the sun and touched the voice of the rain. They had learned from this the art of instant translation. From sense to sense. From self to self." Buckler sets himself to the task of turning these perceptions into words. He tells you not what things are like, but what they are. It is a task that only the great artist can realize.

I believe this to be one of the important Canadian books of this century. Canadians have few masterpieces; this is surely one. Intensely regional, it is none the less a book of universal appeal. It reaches down to touch everybody's dream of a world of beauty, when we were "green and carefree" and "the Sabbath rang holy in the pebbles of the holy stream."

2: MYSTERY AND ORACLE IN ALL THINGS

GREGORY M. COOK

On the strength of two novels, *The Mountain and the Valley* (1952) and *The Cruelest Month* (1963), Ernest Buckler has been described by Claude Bissell as "the subtlest sensibility of contemporary Canadian prose fiction." Similar praise is fully

From "Canadian Books," a review of *Ox Bells and Fireflies* by Gregory M. Cook. In *The Dalhousie Review* 48 (Autumn 1968), 413-14.

justified by his third book, *Ox Bells and Fireflies,* although some queries may arise as to the purely fictional quality of the work, subtitled "A Memoir."

While his ostensibly "non-fiction" book was in progress, Buckler said that the aim was "to give a comprehensive picture, descriptive and analytical, of Nova Scotian village life as I witnessed it at the time of my childhood and alter"—a way of life that "has now vanished forever. I should like to triangulate it, so to speak, within the mingling stream of heritage, material change and social mutation." Buckler has achieved this purpose with the novelist's technique, using fact, incident, and character as "the prism of theme," while subordinating the autobiographical elements to the objective general portrait he offers of "Norstead" (the fictional name of his "no more place"). So the subtitle really is a ploy of the novelist.

Ox Bells and Fireflies is the culmination of both the man and the novelist's principal motivation: the need for a human equation that would express the essence of time and place and that would reconcile the "rustic" and the "more sophisticated" man. The significance of this reconciliation is gradually revealed to the reader, in the twenty-one varieties of subtly textured chapters, as he realizes that what he is sharing with one of the most articulate of English prose stylists is the many-faceted way of life of the rustics, who "however inchoate their expression sometimes was . . . were as charged with depths and intricacies of thought and feeling as the more sophisticated."

The "non-fiction" approach frees the novelist from some of his limitations. The intensely possessive narrator of the first novel is at work, but not at such an unrelieved high pitch and unrelenting immediacy as before. The analytical narrator who nurtured the "more sophisticated" characters (who explored and discovered themselves in the second novel and appear there only parenthentically to keep the "memoir" in a context that is not merely "wispily elegiac") is also employed. The first novel came to grips with the *flesh* translating itself; the second was an examination of the *bones* of life (in the intellectual sense); *Ox Bells and Fireflies* is a contemplative record of the *spirit* of "the way it was." The style is generally more relaxed and casual, but the perception is clear and the insight sudden. This is the magic of memory's "second chance": "The heart, far less misty-eyed than the mind, despite its sentimental name, is far sounder witness. Once in a while it leaps of its own accord —through the skin, through the flesh, through the bone— straight back to the pulse of another time, and takes all of you with it." With the rhythm varied by the use of the first, second, and third point of view, the book's structure and the reader's immediacy are paced expertly after the fashion of memory. At times the speaker in the narrative, like the speaker in a poem (for the book is a prose-poem), seems to take the reader by the hand in Whitmanesque fashion. There is a feeling that "he who touches this book touches a man." But Buckler is not merely a namer, sharing in the act of creation, like Adam or the "Child That Went Forth"; his customary strength of simile and juxtaposed clusters of imagery evoke from the reader constellations of thought and feeling and from the narrator whispers or shouts: "I have created it—I see the oracle in it."

The book is a continuing counterpoint of sadness and joy, life and death, reverence and vigorous humour, told from the child's, the man's, and the woman's point of view. By tapping memory, Buckler has tapped what seems to be a bottomless wellspring of the crowning moments of a lifetime, including "the man's knowing that for each saving instant that brimmed him whole his wife had one of her own."

One moment the young boy leaps with the "unexpected fireflies of what could only be called pure joy" where there is no "moth of disenchantment in any fold of the cloth of the day." When everything seems like "instant Zen" and each day in a child's life a drug to each night's dreams, there is a note of warning: "The world outside, and its sour lessons, could wait." The next moment the adult spectrum (discovered outside Norstead) is summed up: "The whole world is stonestruck because there is nothing listening to *all* of it at once." There are the "bull's-eyes" of conversation, anecdote, and character sketches (forty-eight in one chapter). A man might see the

ceremony of death in a glance at the farm where the dead lay
and "maybe then his sight would blur with that strangest of
human answers, the globe of a tear." At the conclusion of the
funeral, "when for the space of a breath held each face lost its
running total and collided with its own eyes," and then, when
the ritual was over, "A kind of freedom welled up in everyone."
By the final chapter, "Fireflies and Freedom," the narrator has
shared this welling-up with the reader.

Ox Bells and Fireflies is fashioned with a deep love for
those in whom neither the good nor the bad was counterfeit.
So Buckler surpasses himself not only by translating experience,
but by finding the mystery and oracle in all things without
yielding to the sentimental and the nostalgic. He purges himself
and his work of these pitfalls by objective clarification, judg-
ment, and universal statement.

3:   DEEP POOL OF RECOGNITION

LISELOTTE BERLINER

. . . In the afternoon, a Bible sun blazes once through lemon
clouds. And later, blood-red Old Testament towers and firma-
ments burn colder than ice along the horizon.

. . . .

[The people] could seem as cheaply comic as "stage Irish-
men" and as finely strung as pain of death. Their faces could
be as scraggy as turnip knurls or as handsome as apples. . . .
They might be a thing and its contrary at the same time . . .
Sometimes as rough as oaths, they yet had a kind of poetry—
if poetry can be taken as the bottom skin of whatever in all its
differences is all itself . . . But they were always intensely
alive. As, it seemed, were all the things around them. Surely

From a review of *Ox Bells and Fireflies,* by Liselotte Berliner. In
British Columbia Library Journal 32 April (1969), pp. 19-21. By permission of Liselotte Berliner.

the trees exulted and sorrowed. Surely the rocks often longed to be rhododendrons. . . .

Ox Bells and Fireflies, which the author describes as a kind of fictional memoir, picks out the people, places, thoughts and moods of his novel *The Mountain and the Valley* and translates them into poetic gems which are infinitely quotable and totally true. The fact that these multi-faceted ingredients could be welded into a tight, solid novel published eighteen years ago, shows that they are an integral part of Ernest Buckler, who has the artist's magic gift to play with them or on them.

This magician of word and thought seems a fairly ordinary man on the surface. Born of Nova Scotia farmers, rooted in the land, he is a farmer with an M.A. degree in philosophy from the University of Toronto. His first novel, *The Mountain and the Valley,* was published in 1952, *The Cruelest Month,* which I have not yet read, appeared eleven years later; there were magazine contributions, first prize in a *Maclean's* fiction contest, the 1967 Canadian Centennial medal "for valuable service to the nation" and a Canada Council grant to make *Ox Bells and Fireflies* possible. The farm is Buckler's world in an Oriental sense, with a complete interplay of the inner and outer landscape, the flow of the seasons and the sudden chance happenings, the fusion of good and bad, the flaw that is inherent in every organic and inorganic substance—the yin and yang principles always at work in man and landscape, fully recognized and accepted.

Christmas pageants, funerals, annual pig slaughter, the turnip harvest, these are some of the pieces of the patchwork quilt or jigsaw puzzle, two of the many symbols which Buckler uses so subtly in *The Mountain and the Valley.* It all sounds very ordinary, but Buckler's magic shapes these ingredients into a *Magic Mountain* or *Remembrance of Things Past,* totally unrelated settings, yet basically the same. The Nova Scotia farmers do not have the ability to shape or express their thoughts; they reveal tenderness in the simple act of tying a child's mitten to his sleeve; they show their solidarity when the men step behind the barn to urinate and joke briefly about sex and woman.

The depth of emotion, the sense of doom already inherent in each innocent, natural act create a tension, cathartic as in Greek tragedy, masked by the short, simple words of a non-communicative farmer. And here is the ecstasy and the doom of Malcolm Lowry's *Under the Volcano,* but what setting could be more sober, more different! *The Mountain and the Valley* has a seduction scene in which 13-year-old David tumbles in the grass with a neighbour child who yields because she is his friend; when the children come home, there is a letter from a pen pal, the first letter David has ever received, and the sexual experience and the little girl are immediately forgotten in the excitement over this childish communication.

The plot of *The Mountain and the Valley* is simple, the language is concrete and sparse, but the ingredients are deep and multi-faceted, as they are lovingly exposed in *Ox Bells and Fireflies.* Three children grow up in a warm and happy farm setting. The stable, competent, loving father is killed by a tree he felled. It happened the afternoon of a rare, unresolved misunderstanding with his wife. The mother, shattered, dies of a heart attack; the older son is forced into marriage with an unloved neighbour girl whom he made pregnant, but the baby is lost in a miscarriage and the boy eventually leaves his wife, mother-in-law and the farm land he loved. The younger sister is briefly happy with a city boy, but is widowed during the World War. Her twin brother, David—or perhaps Buckler—grows up with a passion for life and words and sex and travel, scars his head permanently in a foolish accident, remains alone on the farm with the old grandmother, until one day he climbs the magic mountain where after sudden flashes of memory and insight he is buried in a snow storm.

In Buckler's wise and magic hands, this is not a soap opera, or revolt against environment or fate, but the regular cycle of nature and the eternal game of chance. A turnip is a turnip is a turnip. The fresh horse manure really smells, and new wallpaper with the rose pattern is the essence of the home, the way Vermeer painted the universe with his Dutch interiors.

Buckler's doors of perception are wide open, and he has the rare gift of opening those of his readers. I have never been to Nova Scotia or met a Nova Scotia farmer, but I am in each scene, symbol, character. Here is the deep pool of recognition, in which we ultimately find our own reflection. It is exciting to discover Buckler, for he is not well-known, nor is he mentioned among the great names in contemporary Canadian, English or American literature, where he so surely belongs. I hope that *Ox Bells and Fireflies* and *The Mountain and the Valley* will be published in a one-volume edition, for these two linked works represent a truly outstanding literary achievement.

4: EARTHY IDYLL

DESMOND PACEY

The Regional Idyll has a long and, on the whole, honourable history in Canadian writing. In the first and second decades of this century, it was the chief of our prose forms, and included such distinguished examples as L. M. Montgomery's *Anne of Green Gables* and Stephen Leacock's *Sunshine Sketches of a Little Town*. In the twenties and thirties it lingered on chiefly in the *Jalna* novels of Mazo de la Roche. In the last thirty years it has been virtually extinct (although it might be argued that W. O. Mitchell's *Who Has Seen the Wind* was a rare outcropping). Now Ernest Buckler, in this "fictional memoir," has produced a book which seems destined to take its place as one of the classics of its kind.

The persistence of the genre in our literature indicates that it expresses a permanent and to some extent distinguished characteristic of our collective psyche. I think it could be argued that one of the most pervasive features of the Canadian sensibility is our tendency to alternate between the dream and the nightmare, between the hope of an impossible heaven and the

From "Earthy Idyll," by Desmond Pacey. In *Canadian Literature* 40 (Spring 1969), pp. 91-92. By permission of Desmond Pacey.

dread of an all-destructive hell. Certainly this bifocal vision is to be found in our literature of travel and exploration, in the poetry of Lampman, Carman and D. C. Scott, and the more recent verse of Pratt, Scott, and Reaney. In our prose fiction, however, the two reactions exist not so much side by side in the same author as in two parallel but antagonistic traditions: the tradition of pessimistic realism best exhibited by the novels of Grove and the early novels of Callaghan, on the one hand, and the tradition of the regional idyll on the other.

The regional idyll lives by the faith that there is or at least was somewhere—in some Canadian small town or village or outport—a way of life which was finer, simpler, purer, more kindly and more honourable than the rat race which prevails in most parts of our industrial civilization. If this faith is pushed too far the work which results is incredible in its thematic optimism and saccharinely sentimental in its setting and characterization; but if the writer is sufficiently skilful and honest to weave into his predominantly bright-coloured fabric a few contrasting threads of ironic grey or sombre black, the resulting tapestry can be convincing and memorable. This feat is accomplished in *Ox Bells and Fireflies*.

Buckler seeks to bring back into collective memory the life of a Nova Scotia farming community as it existed in the early decades of the present century, and he accomplishes his aim with almost complete success. It *is* an idyllic, at times a frankly sentimental, picture that he gives us, but most of the time it is saved from vapidity by the author's scrupulous fidelity of detail, by his frequent touches of subtle or coarse humour, and by his skill in interpolating patches of earthy realism without spoiling the overall idyllic effect. The characters are for the most part more independent, honourable, industrious and vivacious than they probably were in fact, but they are presented with just enough ironic shading to seem credible in the total context of the book.

It is, in fact, the anecdotes of character which seem to me the best part of the book. The passages which describe rural scenery are evocative enough, but to my taste they are somewhat over-written: one is too conscious of the author trying to find the exact, the unusual word. For example, Buckler describes a snowfall as follows:

The snow eyelashes the tufts of brown grass lingering friendless in the fields and comforts them like a blanket. The plowed land is smoothed white, and each twig on every bush is a white pipe cleaner. There is not a breath of wind. The snow shawls the spruces and ridges the bare branches of the chestnut trees with a white piping.

There the metaphors and similes are laid on too thickly, and distract attention from what is really being described; while the pathetic fallacy in the first sentence pushes the tone past honest sentiment into false sentimentality.

Fortunately, when Buckler turns from such set-pieces of nature description to the telling of anecdotes about people, his style loses its self-consciousness and becomes lithely idiomatic or earthily colloquial:

It was Aunt Lena's double distinction that she played the fiddle and was violently allergic to horse farts. She would arrive, wheezing like a bellows from her twenty mile drive—but brave soul that she was, she never failed to oblige us with "Beautiful Isle of Somewhere" before getting her head down on the squaw-weed pillow that was the only real, or fancied, remedy for her condition. Each fall we youngsters scoured the pasture for a fresh supply of the knobby squaw-weed blossoms against just this emergency.

Indeed, an ear for the rich idioms of folk speech is one of the best features of Buckler's book.

5: REMINISCENT SKETCHES

D. O. SPETTIGUE

Ernest Buckler's third book is close to his first, *The Mountain and the Valley* (1952), and so confirms him in the tradition

From a review of *Ox Bells and Fireflies*, by D. O. Spettigue. In *Quarry*, Vol. 18 No. 3 (Summer 1969), pp. 53-54. By permission of D. O. Spettigue.

of reminiscent sketches forming a rural idyll. There is nothing startling about this; no tradition is more indigenous to Canadian literature. But few such books have the solid intellectual base that, without intruding itself, informs *Ox Bells and Fireflies*. (Wallace Stegner's *Wolf Willow* is the only other one to compare, and still the edge is with Mr. Buckler.)

"Scratch a Canadian," Judy LaMarsh has said, "and you find a little place in the country." "Scratch" may not go deep enough, but at least the direction is right, for the essence of Buckler's vision and of his style is the revelation of an inside world, the self for which the outside world is a mirror image. Happiness is their correlation when inside comes out to meet outside as, in spring, "For the first time, outside-the-kitchen and inside-the-kitchen meet, hands out, at the open door." Misery, which appears by a projection in time, is the self locked inside and unable to reach out:

Waves of something benevolent and dissolving of all solemnity come out of everything, as if each thing was its own god-parent. (Not yet—not for a long time yet—the faintest premonition of that later gust which comes from other objects when the brand of parting or of buried chances smokes inside you . . . when "with" has become "without" forever and it comes at you from the missing letter in the swinging metal sign . . . [and] the feet of two small turtles clutch stuporously for footholds on each other, not knowing each other from rocks . . . .)

Time is the villain of every piece, is in fact the imprisoning envelope from which the self would break free. But because Mr. Buckler's, like all such writing, is reminiscent, escape can only be to the past, toward that idyllic childhood when time is Now and place is Here and "from every detail of everything I look at comes the sudden exclamation of its falling exultantly into place within me." But the way from the dead present to the living past is not, as Leacock would have it, via the Mariposa train of memory. Remembering is an intellectual process and Mr. Buckler, like many deep thinkers, is anti-intellectual in the sense that he sees the fundamentals of life as being instinctive, intuitive, beyond reason. Specifically, memory is seen as a function of the active mind and so its recollections are less real than those inexplicable translations by which the present and the past momentarily unite. Mr. Buckler's books are the examination and the celebration of that mysterious transcending of time by which the people of the village and the neighbouring farms, his family and ancestors, even the more distant past of storied Annapolis and his native Nova Scotia can exist simultaneously with the present. "Down we went," as Eliot says, but we can still at intervals catch glimpses of the garden. And these moments of relived past are real, as conscious recall is not.

And though memory may be a miracle—that you can sit where you are and send the mind skimming back over the rails of time and space at will—there's no denying that it can be harping, misleading, and treacherously sentimental. That it often conjures all sorts of things into a vanished way of life that were never there to begin with. (Especially when a writer's mind dives back into his country childhood. . . .) The heart, far less misty-eyed than the mind, despite its sentimental name, is a far sounder witness. Once in a while it leaps of its own accord —through the skin, through the flesh, through the bone— straight back to the pulse of another time, and takes all of you with it. You are not seeing this place again through the blurred telescope of the mind: you are standing right there.

And of course the triumph of Mr. Buckler's prose is that it puts you "right there":

I mean, you'd be standing there on the bank of the brook . . . . The sun would be drowsing on your back. Sounds themselves would have a little pocket of stillness around them like rocks have. Your fishing line would be hanging slack from the alder pole into the pondlike stillwater. And then suddenly the surge of a trout would stretch your line taut and all at once your heart would seem to spread out like a fan and you would know exactly what trout*ness* was, And *brook*ness. And *leaf*ness. And, yes, *world*ness and *life*ness itself. You would move right out— and gloriously—into everything around you.

IMAGERY AND SYMBOLISM

The writer can guide you and, if he describes a hovel, make it seem the symbol of social injustice and provoke your indignation. The painter is mute. He presents you with a hovel, that's all. You are free to see in it what you like. That attic window will never be the symbol of misery; for that, it would have to be a sign, whereas it is a thing.[1]

Jean-Paul Sartre

In David Canaan's life Buckler presents, through symbolic technique, an inevitable, ironic tragedy. Man, an impermanent, insignificant being operates in an indifferent universe where he seeks to establish a static self through human relationships of family and community. This static self soothes the conscience and gives meaning to life. Occasionally, however, there appears in life a highly sensitive individual who, through misfortune of time and place, finds himself in a less sensitive society and is unable to participate in every-day human relationships. For this individual the creative desire remains physically unfulfilled and the result is isolation, loneliness and, for David Canaan, sacrifice. David goes to the grave with his hopes and expectations materially unfulfilled.

The Mountain and the Valley is not conventional tragedy in the high mimetic sense since David lacks the heroic proportions of either the tragic hero or tragic leader and, therefore, is not isolated from society through action. David is not a Lear, an

From "The Mountain and the Valley: A Study in Canadian Fiction," by Ian A. Atkinson. An unpublished Master's thesis, English, 1969a, The Library, University of Guelph. Portions of Chapter II and "Conclusion" are included here, pp. 57-58, 77-81. By permission of I. A. Atkinson.

[1] Jean-Paul Sartre, *What is Literature?* trans. Bernard Frechtman (New York: Harper Colophon Books, 1965), p. 4.

Othello, or a Macbeth. Nor is *The Mountain and the Valley* simple, low mimetic tragedy: David Canaan has no pathetic obsession to be sacrificed. Buckler's novel follows the tradition of inevitable tragic irony which is a refinement of the low mimetic.

Tragic irony . . . becomes simply the study of tragic isolation as such, and it thereby drops out the element of the special case, which in some degree is in all the other modes. Its hero does not necessarily have any tragic hamartia or pathetic obsession: he is only somebody who gets isolated from his society. Thus the central principle of tragic irony is that whatever exceptional happens to the hero should be casually out of line with his character. Tragedy is intelligible, not in the sense of having any pat moral to go with it, but in the sense that Aristotle had in mind when he spoke of discovery or recognition as essential to the tragic plot. Tragedy is intelligible because its catastrophe is plausibly related to its situation. Irony isolates from the tragic situation the sense of arbitrariness, of the victim's having been unlucky, selected at random or by lot, and no more deserving of what happens to him than anyone else would be. If there is a reason for choosing him for catastrophe, it is an inadequate reason and raises more objections than it answers.[2]

David is what Frye refers to as the *pharmakos* or scapegoat— the Hester Prynne, the Billy Budd, the Tess, the Septimus Lucretius Ward or the Ishmael figure.

The *pharmakos* is neither innocent nor guilty. He is innocent in the sense that what happens to him is far greater than anything he has done provokes, like the mountaineer whose shout brings down an avalanche. He is guilty in the sense that he is a member of a guilty society, or living in a world where such injustices are an inescapable part of existence. The two facts do not come together; they remain ironically apart. The *pharmakos,* in short, is in the situation of Job. Job can defend himself against the charge of having done something that makes his

---

[2] Northrop Frye, *Anatomy of Criticism* Princeton, N.J.: Princeton University Press, 1957), p. 41.

catastrophe morally intelligible; but the success of his defense makes it morally unintelligible.[3]

Through no fault of his own, David is thrown into a society that lives a less intense life than his own. Consequently, society forces him to a sufficient degree of inaction to turn him to the imaginative future. As a result he sinks to physical acts that cannot be justified by social standards and rises to heights of imaginative creation that can be understood only by himself. Buckler's tone is neither bitter nor harsh. David feels he has been cheated in life during "The Train" section, but this feeling of loss is overcome in the imagination where all things are possible. There are no turns along the road where David's life could have been different. This is stressed in the apparent determinism that governs not only David's life but the lives of all the major characters in the novel.

For Buckler, life is a recurring cyclic process that denies man a comprehension of death. Meaning in life is fabricated through a sense of history, a sense of family, and a sense of human relationships all of which produce a pattern of man's continuance. Even the apparent ending of the Canaan family (there is no birth in the novel) is acceptable since evidence of their existence is found in Ellen's rugs. Each event is carefully hooked into memory by a provocative piece of cloth that stirs the consciousness of the concerned individuals. Once this stream of consciousness is eclipsed by death, life ceases to be a struggle and the evidence then reiterates the universal pattern of man's existence.

Although Buckler portrays the tragedy of David Canaan, he is unable to explain the choice of victim. Perhaps for this reason God is not significant in the novel. Buckler symbolically provides his balm for human suffering in the Faith-Hope-Love tableau of the concert but the community ignores the prescription.

In plotting a life from youth to death, something Canadian fiction has been hesitant to do, Buckler captures, through sym-

---

[3] *Ibid.*, pp. 41-42.

bolic technique in structure, imagery, character and dream, the psychological pattern of a life that witnesses initiation, love, death, alienation, dissolution of family, external destruction of dreams, desertion of land, urbanization, war and scientific revolution. During David's thirty years, a new highway is constructed through the valley and the automobile becomes a common sight, yet as life races by on steel and pavement, David, the artist-in-exile, struggles on with oxen and horses in a manner reminiscent of a hero in a novel by Hardy or Lawrence.

The fact that David's life ends on the mountain strongly suggests the crucifixion. Like Christ, David has no real father since he is never able to identify with Joseph; in another sense he is Moses, the man who leads the artist out of exile through a form of self-sacrifice, and in still another light he is the Ishmael figure, visibly recognized by his mark of Cain (scar) as the doomed outcast.

In Canadian literary history, *The Mountain and the Valley* will probably be viewed as one of the major novels responsible for bringing to an end the stereotyped hero and heroine of the "valley" novel, and for introducing a more complicated, realistic anti-hero and anti-heroine through David and Anna. *The Mountain and the Valley* might also be recognized as a novel that successfully probes and explodes familial and societal myths in an effort to expose life as it is and perhaps improve upon it.

. . . .

Buckler creates his myth by symbolically portraying a people he knows well. Like Hardy's Wessex folk they speak the uncomplicated local dialect of a basically oral society. For this reason the prose has a metaphysical composition that gains its analogy from the local color of the everyday events in their lives. Consequently, by virtue of Buckler's honest portrayal, it is their own myth. Buckler discards or destroys erroneous conceptions that portray the ceaseless conflict between man and nature or the eternally happy village; he symbolically builds a myth that expresses man's frustrations and longings. He avoids stereotypes and tries to realistically capture the characters and institutions of life. Some of his portrayals may resemble archetypes of the "valley" novel but, in fact, they are complex, realistic portrayals that encompass the tragic myth of the isolated artist. The purpose of the myth is to release the long-suffocated potential of Canadian fiction. It is only through awareness of man's suffering that man's artistic creativity is brought to full bloom. In *The Birth of Tragedy,* Nietzsche says: "Without myth . . . every culture loses its healthy creative natural power: it is only a horizon encompassed with myths that rounds off to unity a social movement."[4]

There is little else in Canadian fiction that readily lends itself to comparison with Buckler's carefully developed myth of the sacrificed artist. Such images and symbols as the talismanic revolver in *Swamp Angel,* the lake in *The Apprenticeship of Duddy Kravitz,* or the canoe in *The Watch That Ends the Night* are an ancillary part of their works and offer no rewarding comparison with Buckler's myth-forming imagery and symbolism. Buckler's myth of the sacrificed artist is best paralleled in Irving Layton's poem, "The Birth of Tragedy," which was written two years after *The Mountain and the Valley.* I quote the last stanza:

> A quiet madman, never far from tears,
> I lie like a slain thing
> under the green air the trees
> inhabit, or rest upon a chair
> towards which the inflammable air
> tumbles on many robins' wings;
> noting how seasonably
> leaf and blossom uncurl
> and living things arrange their death,
> while someone from afar off
> blows birthday candles for the world.[5]

---

[4] Friedrich Nietzsche, *The Birth of Tragedy,* trans. Clifton P. Fadiman in *The Philosophy of Nietzsche,* (New York, 1969), p. 168.

[5] Carl F. Klinck and Reginald E. Watters, *Canadian Anthology* (revised ed.; Toronto: W. J. Gage Ltd., 1966), p. 387.

ON *OX BELLS AND FIREFLIES*

JOHN C. ORANGE

At the end of *The Mountain and the Valley* David looks over the valley and he sees the "neglected warmth" in everything and everyone. He decides that someday he will write about all he has known, just the way it was [p. 300], and in some ways *Ox Bells and Fireflies* is the novel that is dormant inside of him.

Buckler himself has called it " a memoir sometimes cast in imaginative form; the kind of novelistic non-fiction on which I think Capote is quite wrong in his claim to have registered the first patent."[1] This book characteristically opens with a narrator (Mark) recalling his childhood, and the whole second chapter is devoted to "Memory." This narrator is again one who is both part of his story and yet free to enter into everyone's sensibilities (including the reader's). He ranges in and out of first, second and third person points of view. In choosing a "fictional memoir" form, Buckler has been able to sidestep the problems of structure that plagued his too obviously "constructed" second novel.

This is not to say that the book has no structure at all, however. It begins when "Time is young" and "I had never seen a dead person,"[2] and generally it moves ahead in "real time" through school, work, puberty, marriage, parenthood, neighbours, and ends once again with childhood.

From "The Masks of the Artist" by John C. Orange. An unpublished Master of Philosophy essay, English, University of Toronto Library. Chapter V, pp. 86-93. By permission of John C. Orange.

[1] University of Toronto Library, Buckler Collection, letter from Ernest Buckler to Miss J. Rogers, June 30, 1967.

[2] Ernest Buckler, *Ox Bells and Fireflies,* (Toronto: McClelland and Stewart Ltd., 1968) p. 3. All subsequent references are taken from this edition and indicated in brackets in the text itself.

One interesting aspect of this pattern is that although "real (chronological) time" is *linear,* the child of the last chapter is the *same* child as in the first, so that "memory time," and the time contained by the book itself, are *circular.* "Thematic time" may be a useful term in describing how "real time" transcends itself to become "circular time." In the superficial narrative line of the book, the narrator seems to be describing his own development in a specific place, inside a specific span of time— Nova Scotia more than fifty years ago. The way the narrator *treats* his personal development, however, is by making everything "stand for many"—by arranging his chapters in a *thematic* sequence that parallels his use of chronological or "real time." Each of the twenty-one chapters deals with an aspect of life (youthful pranks, games, myths, food, work, rooms in houses, courtship and marriage, money, mail, parental attitudes, eccentric neighbours, community fellow-feeling and countless others) that occurs to everyone in one way or another. Each chapter contains "universals" general enough to remain afloat on the multitude of particular images used to describe their emotional qualities. In this way the book has *universal* appeal, and yet, at the same time, it possesses an intensely *local* flavour. Norstead, the "no more place" becomes a microcosm for a "no more time"—a lost (or at least vanishing) way of life. One can't help thinking at the same time, however, that Buckler has captured those aspects of life—family bonds, pictures of real beauty, responses to change, shyness and laughter, sorrow and elation, the psychology of eccentrics, the wonder of things, the mystery of death—that will *never* really change. Hence the cyclic "memory time" becomes fused with "thematic time," and the book's form and the author's techniques (of style and construction) can be seen as inseparable.

This work, rather than *The Mountain and the Valley,* serves to show that the country people's "peaks of peculiarly vivid happiness" actually balance the hardships of their lives. But, as in the earlier book, the light reflected by nature contains the ineluctable spectre of death. Ox bells consistently represent sorrow while fireflies stand for freedom. The book begins with youth "the night before death" [p. 4], and although time seems to move ahead toward death, the last lines of the book are "And fireflies and freedom." [p. 302] Time has passed, but it has moved no further than the hands of a clock.

His method of organization allows Buckler all the freedom he needs to accommodate his imaginative style. Once again the narrator can roam his rural Eden discovering its wonders, and by translating each thing's special light into words, he "creates" all things (see p. 298). Light gives each created thing its own "shaft of clarity":

Light, finding things, draws their shadows from them slantwise on the ground, then gives them light. The tin pails shine. Diamonds are discovered in the pebbles of the road, emeralds in the branch tips of the firs, rubies in the idol eyes of roosters, ebony in the black horse's glistening flank. Dandelions dazzle themselves with yellow. Shingles glow gray, with fatherly knowledge. Thistles sparkle with a family wit. Spider bridges, cantilevered as light as glances, twinkle between the plum tree twigs. Auntly hens shine brown on the glinting straw. Swallows shimmer, hills kindle, and the fields sheen themselves with resurrection and internal rhyme . . . . Kingfishers bright as rings draw perfect parabolas on the air and sing of them. Clocks brighten at the thought of company, the bread knife awakens, and plates become transitive. A hush of freshness walks on the air like Christ. [pp. 8, 9]

There is a rejoicing in the proliferation of things, almost in Whitmanesque fashion—except that Buckler's poetic prose usually contains more poetic devices than Whitman's prose poems do. Abstract and concrete images fuse to form conceits— shingles with fatherly knowledge, thistles with wit, webs as light as glances, hills feeling their own internal rhyme, plates becoming transitive, are excellent examples of Buckler's unique imaginative vision. His use of personification is characteristic, as is his choice of onomatopoetic verbs, phonetic intensives, alliterations, and startling metaphors such as "idol eyes of roosters" and "auntly hens." Kingfishers singing of the parabolas they draw in the air is a characteristic example of Buckler's preference for mathematical images. These aid him in his fusion of the "realities" of the concrete and the abstract and it is this quality that gives his style its metaphysical flavour. Once again, the author searches for the phrase of illumination contained within each thing that forms an equation with some human feeling—and ultimately with all other things. The artist's job seems to be to find "a thing's light," focus it through the lens of memory which then translates it into feeling.

No single description can contain them. . . . everything, animate or inanimate, cast a different shadow of itself as its context varied. [pp. 19, 20]

. . . .

. . . each and every form of existence was there in its own translation. [p. 20]

. . . .

And though memory may be a miracle . . . . The heart, far less misty-eyed than the mind, despite its sentimental name, is a far sounder witness. Once in a while it leaps of its own accord—through the skin, through the flesh, through the bone—straight back to the pulse of another time, and takes all of you with it . . . . not long enough to take it all down, but long enough to give memory a second chance. [p. 21]

One of Buckler's favourite anagrams is that "heart" and "earth" have the same letters. Clearly the artist's sensitivities into the special light of things involve an intuitive process in which the heart is focused through the lens of memory. Time is the shutter which allows special light to enter only for a blinding instant, and the result is a series of very clear and very special photographic effects:

The snow eyelashes the tufts of brown grass. [p. 4]

. . . .

I can see that this is a day when Father and Mother too like to keep the perimeter of their presences touching. [p. 10]

. . . .

Nearer the house, the wild crabapple tree foams with blossoms and bees intent as theologians. [p. 26]

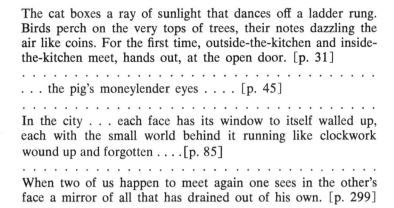

The cat boxes a ray of sunlight that dances off a ladder rung.
Birds perch on the very tops of trees, their notes dazzling the
air like coins. For the first time, outside-the-kitchen and inside-
the-kitchen meet, hands out, at the open door. [p. 31]

. . . .
. . . the pig's moneylender eyes . . . . [p. 45]

. . . .
In the city . . . each face has its window to itself walled up,
each with the small world behind it running like clockwork
wound up and forgotten . . . . [p. 85]

. . . .
When two of us happen to meet again one sees in the other's
face a mirror of all that has drained out of his own. [p. 299]

Buckler's garden is, again characteristically, by no means a
preternatural one. Death is a recurring motif in the midst of
spring and ecstasy. Mark's earliest memory is of the day of a
funeral, and the very centre of the book is devoted to a description of Death's "great sabled presence." The incantation of the
crows begins in sorrow and ends with "a secret never to be
told." This child's rhyme is a chorus that recurs throughout the
book calling up associations of the black bird and the secret.
In two chapters devoted to anecdotes about various neighbours,
some of the most amusing, warm, stories end abruptly when the
character suddenly dies (Chapters 19 and 20).

This book contrasts city and country life even more explicitly
than the other two novels do. The city always represents a
place of endless repetition, sterility, automatons. Written from a
1968 vantage point, Buckler obviously uses his contrasts as
warnings. He always implies that the life he is describing is
vanishing forever, and that it has been replaced by city life
which is always described in negative terms. This has a double
effect in the same way that the pervading spirit of death does.
It tones down the rapture of the whole book, but heightens
individual moments in it. In this way all of Buckler's writing
is saved from being too nostalgic or sentimental.

The narrator's frustrating artistic problems have become notes
in short parentheses in this novel:

(Not yet the compulsion to think hard. Not yet the discovery that too much thought about things stirs them up, until they dismay you with their infinite clamor.) [p. 37]

He is nevertheless still dissatisfied with his art as a means of adequately capturing life and translating accurately: "A man putting the dipper of clear sap to his mouth in the maple grove in the morning dew alert as a partridge (while all over the world the ink rusts on the paper)." [p. 201] Once again the tension between an intuitive view of life and a distrust of words to communicate this view results in a kind of prose that is obsessed with clarification.

COPY OF A LETTER TO ANGUS CAMERON

HARRY BROWN

1 January 1969

For Angus Cameron

When I ordered Ernest Buckler's *Ox Bells and Fireflies* it was because of a mild and dispassionate curiosity about the Nova Scotia of a half-century ago. This, the subject of the Buckler book, is also the place where my father and maternal grandmother were born and raised. I have not been there since I was a very small boy, on a visit I no longer recall. So, as might be surmised. I ordered the book in a somewhat offhand way. And then—

Well, I had caught a Tartar, and no mistake. Instead of finding myself with a mild volume of boyhood reminiscences, suitable for my mild interest, I had read but a few pages of Buckler's first chapter when I was sent sprawling by the first of a series of emotional hammer-blows that kept sending me to the canvas again whenever I struggled to my knees and, after I'd regretfully reached the end of the book, left me dazed for a solid week.

Ernest Buckler hasn't merely written about some people who lived, and some things that happened, in Nova Scotia in the early Twentieth Century; what he's done is set down as beautifully compassionate, as awesomely moving, a study of our human universals and eternals as I have ever read. Or, I daresay, could bear to read again—for such is the almost unbearable compactness of this book that it should give every man his life's worth of emotional intensity.

Copy of a letter to Angus Cameron from Harry Brown. In a personal letter to Ernest Buckler from Harry Brown (January 1, 1969). By permission of Harry Brown.

Now, I'm not in the habit of whipping off mash-notes to those precious few, the writers whose books bowl me over. For one thing, I've spent too much time with too many writers, singly or in groups, to want to break in a pedestalizing act this late in the performance, let alone with a straight face; and for another thing, damned few books have managed to bowl me over, anyway. Ernest Buckler, however, gave me no choice: I had to tell him how stunned, slack-jawed and, let's face it, envious I was by the time I'd finished his *Ox Bells and Fireflies*. The book, by God, is a classic; incipient now, maybe—but just wait a decade or so. You'll see.

If, after telling Buckler how I felt, I'm expected to add that I wish I could also tell every literate person in the U.S. and Canada the same thing—well, I'd hate to be hanging until *that* particular expectation came true. When it comes to books as fine as this one, literacy is not enough. The Average Reader, so-called, simply lacks the sensitivity, as well as sufficient spiritual reserves, to be allowed to read this latest work of Mr. Buckler.

BIBLIOGRAPHICAL NOTE

NOVELS BY ERNEST BUCKLER

The Mountain and the Valley. New York: Henry Holt & Co., 1952.

————. New York: New American Library, 1954.

————. Toronto: McClelland and Stewart, 1961, and successive reprints.

The Cruelest Month. Toronto: McClelland and Stewart, 1963.

Ox Bells and Fireflies. Toronto: McClelland and Stewart, 1968.

————. New York: Alfred A. Knopf, 1968.

SHORT STORIES AND EXCERPTS FROM NOVELS BY ERNEST BUCKLER have been published in: *Esquire, Saturday Night, Colliers, Ladies' Home Journal, MacLean's, Chatelaine, Weekend, Better Farming, Atlantic Advocate, Canadian Home Journal, Reader's Digest* and numerous anthologies.

ARTICLES AND REVIEWS BY ERNEST BUCKLER have appeared in: *Esquire, Saturday Night, Coronet, Quill and Quire, Maclean's, The Atlantic Monthly, The Atlantic Advocate, Farm Journal, Fiddlehead, New York Times Book Review, Los Angeles Times Book Review* and in several newspapers.

POEMS, RADIO SCRIPTS, TRANSLATIONS AND OTHER MANUSCRIPTS have been catalogued as part of the Buckler Collection in the Archives, University of Toronto Library.

DATE DUE
DATE DE RETOUR
